Cultural alternatives and a feminist anthropology

Cultural alternatives and a feminist anthropology

An analysis of culturally constructed gender interests in Papua New Guinea

Frederick Errington

Five College Professor of Anthropology
Mount Holyoke College

Deborah Gewertz

Professor, Amherst College

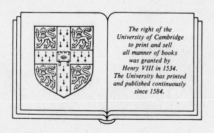

The right of the
University of Cambridge
to print and sell
all manner of books
was granted by
Henry VIII in 1534.
The University has printed
and published continuously
since 1584.

Cambridge University Press
Cambridge
New York   Port Chester
Melbourne   Sydney

Published by the Press Syndicate of the University of Cambridge
The Pitt Building, Trumpington Street, Cambridge, CB2 1RP
40 West 20th Street, New York, NY 10011, USA
10 Stamford Road, Oakleigh, Melbourne 3166, Australia

First published 1987
First paperback edition 1989

Printed in Great Britain at the University Press Cambridge

British Library cataloguing in publication data

Errington, Frederick Karl.
Cultural alternatives and a feminist anthropology:
an analysis of culturally constructed gender
interests in Papua New Guinea.
1. Ethnology – Papua New Guinea – Chambri.
2. Sex role – Papua New Guinea – Chambri.
I. Title. II. Gewertz, Deborah B.
305.3'0899912   GN671.N5

Library of Congress cataloguing in publication data

Errington, Frederick Karl.
Cultural alternatives and a feminist anthropology.
Bibliography.
Includes index.
1. Chambri (Papua New Guinea people) – Social life and customs.
2. Sex role – Papua New Guinea.
I. Gewertz, Deborah B., 1948–   . II. Title.
DU740.42.E77 1987   306'.09953   86-26823

ISBN 0 521 33492 6 hard covers
ISBN 0 521 37591 6 paperback

CE

To
Carolyn Errington
and
Frederica Goldsmith

Contents

Illustrations

Acknowledgments

We thank those institutions which provided the assistance necessary for the completion of this book. The Department of Anthropology in the Research School of Pacific Studies of the Australian National University supported us during 1983–84 and sponsored our two-month field trip to Papua New Guinea during 1983. Gewertz has made two previous trips to the Chambri. From 1974 through 1975, she was supported by the Population Institute of the East-West Center, the National Geographic Society and the Graduate School of the City University of New York. The second trip, during the summer of 1979, was sponsored by the National Endowment for the Humanities and by Amherst College. Gratitude is also expressed to the Wenner-Gren Foundation for Anthropological Research, which enabled her to investigate archival material during 1981.

Many individuals also contributed to the completion of this project. Among those who deserve special mention for their helpful comments on various portions of our manuscript are the following members of the group invited to the Australian National University by the Department of Anthropology in the Research School of Pacific Studies to study "Gender relations in the Southwestern Pacific: ideology, politics and production": Leslie Haviland, Terence Hays, Janet Hoskins, Roger Keesing, Martha Macintyre, Jill Nash, Marie Reay, Marilyn Strathern, James Weiner and Michael Young. In addition, Jan Dizard, Jerome Himmelstein, James Rothenberg and Eleanor Vander Haegen provided us with important sociological perspectives.

We would also like to thank the cartographers at the Research School of Pacific Studies for their maps and diagrams. We also appreciate the support, humor and friendship we received from Ann

Buller, Helen Collins, Ita Pead, Judith Wilson and Ria van de Zandt.

We are particularly indebted to Eleanor Leacock and Fitz John Porter Poole for their most thorough and helpful comments on the manuscript as a whole. We are also extremely grateful to Carolyn Errington for her invaluable editorial assistance.

Our greatest debt is to the Chambri people. To Anton Bascom, Schola and Francis Imbang, Lakindimi, Pekur, Matias and Bridgit Yambumpe, Sapui Yapundipi, Patrick Yarapat and, of course, to our old friend, Andrew Yorondu, we owe special thanks.

Finally, we wish to note at the outset of this book that the order in which our names appear as authors has been determined by alphabetical consideration alone.

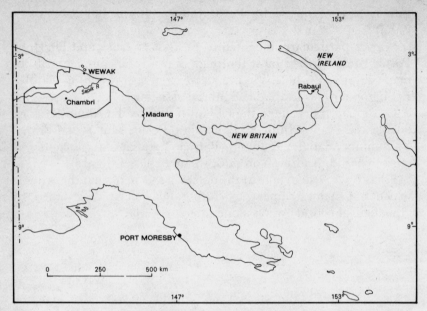

Map 1.   The Chambri of the East Sepik Province of Papua New Guinea

Introduction
The promise of cultural alternatives

Anthropologists necessarily must be conscious of their own personal and cultural identity when they do research in societies with exotic cultures. Their emotional and intellectual predispositions constitute perspectives which are sources both of misinterpretation and – as bases of contrast – of analytic clarity.[1] It is hard to imagine an instance in which the relationship between the perspective held by an anthropologist and the socio-cultural "reality" under examination is more complex than in this present study. We are two anthropologists, a husband and wife, examining male–female relationships among a people, the Chambri (see Map 1), whom another husband and wife team, Reo Fortune and Margaret Mead, studied, and who were made famous by Mead as the "Tchambuli" – a society in which women dominated over men.

A Chambri artifact with a curious history has come to embody much of this complexity for us. Shortly before we were to leave Chambri in early 1984, we were talking to Andrew Yorondu, Deborah Gewertz's best friend and informant during her two previous field trips, about his experiences during World War II. While Frederick Errington was preparing to play back the recording just made of Yorondu's account, Deborah jokingly told the old man that some of his personal history had already been inscribed. To demonstrate, she began reading from her copy of Reo Fortune's unpublished field notes. There, Fortune describes a ceremony for the validation of a war canoe which he and Margaret Mead had observed in 1933 while they lived among the Chambri. We read to Yorondu about "Yauranda, the nine or ten year old son of Kwoli-kumbi [who] chew[ed] betel nut and lime standing in the canoe at the stern and looking out sternward."[2] We continued about how he was to spit the betel nut juice onto a *talimbun* shell (a green snail

1

shell, *Turbo marmoratus*) which had been placed in the prow and then call the canoe's name, but the "child was abashed by so many spectators and remained silent – so that others about announced the name as if the child had said it" (Fortune, 1933a).

Yorondu was delighted by this excursion into his past and with evident amusement completed the story of his childhood embarrassment. He had, it seems, been so mortified by his incapacity to speak that he had fled into the bush, not to return home that night.

When Yorondu visited us the following day, he had, in his turn, a surprise for us: a battered, rusty, trade store hatchet that Fortune had given his father, Kwolikumbi, in exchange for the war trophy of a decorated human skull. Yorondu wanted to give us this hatchet as a farewell gift because, he said, it was fitting that it return to its source.

We do not know whether this gift was to close a relationship or to continue one. It was probably intended to close our relationship because when we said our final goodbyes to each other a few days later he said that on our next visit he would already be dead. In any case, the hatchet conveyed for him much about the nature of his life, particularly as it had been marked by the visits of anthropologists.[3]

We had, of course, previously thought many times about the relationship between the data and analyses of Mead and Fortune and our own. However, Yorondu's gift of the hatchet he had inherited from his father, based on the Chambri perception of us all as comparable Europeans, made us examine the interpersonal link between the two generations of anthropologists. What, after all, did it mean to be the heirs of Reo Fortune and Margaret Mead? And it was again Yorondu who provided the context which encouraged us to think further about this question.

Yorondu had always worked intensively with Deborah on all aspects of Chambri culture. She had sat next to him in his men's house, had tape-recorded his esoteric ritual secrets and had seen all – she thought – of his ritual paraphernalia. She was astonished, therefore, when he invited Frederick, but not her, to see and hear about powerful ritual objects which she had not known existed. On a small table next to the centerpost of his house he normally displayed such items as his radio, his two copies of the Bible, a photograph of him holding a small crocodile (a photograph Deborah had taken of him almost 10 years before), his ceremonial headdress and the lime spatula decorated with feathers, each feather to signify a death for which he took credit. For this occasion,

Photograph 1. Yorondu's shell embossed clay flute

however, he had augmented the usual display with six bamboo flutes, two blackened *talimbun* shells and, as the most sacred object, his shell-embossed clay flute, whose ancestral voice, he said, spoke without human assistance of enemy deaths.

After Deborah protested to Yorondu that she had always been privy to his ritual knowledge, he allowed her to accompany Frederick to this new display. He, however, did send his wife, daughter, and several visiting kinswomen from the house before he explained the significance of these objects to us. These women were far from disconcerted by their exclusion and continued to chat with each other, somewhat bemused by Yorondu's preoccupation with ritual items.

Only Deborah was annoyed. She realized that the exhibition and explanation of these objects would not have taken place without Frederick's presence. But why exactly should this annoy her, we later wondered, when it scarcely even occasioned the notice of Chambri women? Evidently, none of them wished to have access to male ritual knowledge or to otherwise be like the Chambri men.

Nor, on reflection, did Deborah. Nor, for that matter, did Frederick wish to be defined in the manner of Chambri men.

Deborah had been annoyed and Frederick little gratified because, at least on the occasion of Yorondu's revelation, our *fundamental* identity – and, consequently, our access to particular sorts of experience – had been defined in terms of criteria which were both categorical and social. Definition according to such criteria, we felt, discounted our own sense of personal identity, our own sense of individuality. Although, to be sure, we regarded ourselves as having gender, we also were, in our view, a particular man and a particular woman, each of whom had developed (and should be allowed to continue to develop) a set of relatively unique dispositions, capacities and perspectives.[4] Unfortunately, both the criteria through which Chambri men and women are defined and the relative exclusivity of their respective realms became more applicable to us once we entered their social life as a man and a woman. As an anthropologist actively engaging in Chambri social life, Frederick had made Deborah more comprehensible to the Chambri as a woman and wife.[5] But, as her identity became increasingly acceptable to them, it became less so to her.

How ironic, we reflected, that this discovery should take place during field work among the Chambri – where Margaret Mead thought she had observed men waiting on the words of women, an observation, she hoped, that would help American women to change their relationships with men and thus strengthen their own identities. Clearly, we realized from our reactions, neither Chambri men nor women could provide direct models for American men and women. To be the heirs of Fortune and Mead, we now came to realize, meant that we must examine once again those sociocultural arrangements that provided the identity and the experience of Chambri men and women and to reconsider the relationship of those Chambri lives to our own.

When Margaret Mead traveled with Reo Fortune to the East Sepik Province of Papua New Guinea in 1933, her plan was "to study the different ways in which cultures patterned the expected behavior of males and females" (1972: 196). Later that year, settled among the Tchambuli, she began to wonder:

What if human beings, innately different at birth, could be shown to fit into systematically defined temperamental types, and what if there were male and female versions of each of these temperamental types? And what if a society – by the way in which children were reared, by the kinds of behavior that were rewarded or punished, and by its traditional depiction of heroes, heroines, and villains, witches, sorcerers, and supernaturals – could place its major emphasis on one type of temperament, as among the Arapesh or Mundugumor, or could, instead, emphasize a special complementarity among the sexes, as the Iatmul and the Tchambuli did? And what if the expectations about male-female differences, so characteristic of Euro-American cultures, could be reversed, as they seemed to be in Tchambuli, where women were brisk and cooperative, whereas men were responsive, subject to the choices of women, and characterized by the kinds of cattiness, jealousy, and moodiness that feminists had claimed were the outcome of women's subservient and dependent role? (1972: 216)

Her answers to these questions in *Sex and Temperament* (1935) and *Male and Female* (1949) have become widely known to specialists in anthropology and women's studies, as well as to members of the general public, including Deborah's mother, who was given a copy of *Male and Female* in 1952, four years after Deborah was born. She consulted it from time to time until Deborah, a fledgling anthropologist about to embrace Melanesia as her "culture area," appropriated it from her. It was not, however, until we began to write this book, some 12 years after *Male and Female* became Deborah's, that we read carefully the message its donor had inscribed.

In clearing out my overflow of books, I thought you'd like this, Fredi – it helps explain a lot of the stereotyped misconceptions about the "feminine" male types and "masculine" female types – very important in helping to understand young people today, and even those of us who are "older and wiser."

Before she passed the book on, Deborah's mother's friend under-lined the following passage:

A recognition of these possibilities [for flexibility within gender role assignment] would change a great many of our present-day practices of rearing children. We would cease to describe the behaviour of the boy who showed an interest in occupations regarded as female, or a greater sensitivity than his fellows, as "on the female" side, and could ask instead what kind of male he was going to be. We would take instead the primary fact of sex membership as a cross-constitutional classification, just as on a wider scale the fact of sex can be used to classify together male rabbits and male lions and male deer, but would never be permitted to obscure for us their essential rabbit, lion, and deer characteristics. Then the little girl who shows a greater need to take things apart than most of the other little girls need not be classified as a female of a certain kind . . .

If we are to provide the impetus for surmounting the trials and obstacles of this most difficult period in history, man must be sustained by a vision of a future so rewarding that no sacrifice is too great to continue the journey towards it. In that picture of the future, the degree to which men and women can feel at home with their bodies, and at home in their relationships with their own sex and with the opposite sex, is extremely important. (1949: 142)

The trials and obstacles to be faced during the late 1940s, according to Mead, would be those encountered in the attempt to build a global culture in which individuals would have freedom to develop their potentialities (see Mead, 1949: 12–14). Deborah's mother, and many like her, responded by socializing their children in as liberated a fashion as possible. To change the world, they believed, meant changing its children.[6] But this new generation of children, particularly the daughters who had not been classified as "masculine" females and who were encouraged to take things apart, began to unravel the connection between a life of child rearing and a world of personal fulfillment.

Many of these daughters had come to view their mothers as restricted to the suburbs by a capitalist economy needing women as occasional workers and as full-time consumers.[7] These daughters argued that instead of eliminating national and global inequalities, the child-centered existences of their mothers had merely reproduced them.

In yet another way Mead's work on gender roles came to figure importantly in their lives. Their primary interest shifted: whereas they had learned about cross-cultural variation in definitions of male and female so that they could socialize their children to achieve freedom through defining their own gender roles, they now learned from Mead's descriptions of different sociocultural arrangements so that they themselves might achieve freedom through obtaining power hitherto monopolized by men. Among the different societies Mead described, the Chambri had perhaps the most significance for them because within that society, they thought, women exercised power. For instance, Mead had written in *Sex and Temperament*:

For although Tchambuli is patrilineal in organization, although there is polygyny and a man pays for his wife – two institutions that have been popularly supposed to degrade women – it is the women in Tchambuli who have the real position of power in society. The patrilineal system includes houses and land, residence land and gardening-land, but only an occasional particularly energetic man gardens. For food, the people depend upon the fishing of women ... And the most important manufacture, the mosquito-bags, two of which will purchase an ordinary canoe, are made entirely by women ... And women control the proceeds in *kinas* and *talibun*.[8](1935: 253–254)

In Mead's analysis, the power she saw Chambri women as possessing was based on what she interpreted as their economic independence. By analogy, many American women believed, they, too, could achieve their independence if they had their own charge cards and mortgages, as well as banks and businesses. As one of our women colleagues put it: "to balance my own checkbook was, then, of transcendent value." Chambri women appeared to be the consummate checkbook balancers, while Chambri men were forced to ask their wives for spending allowances. Mead's description of Chambri men as catty, moody and jealous was understood to be the outcome of their subservient and dependent positions.

But why then, when Yorondu treated Deborah more as a Chambri woman than he had before, did she, an American women brought up to become as Mead thought Chambri women were, feel subservient and dependent? Our answer, which we have already anticipated, is that a major portion of Mead's analysis of male-female relationships among the Chambri is incorrect. In her effort to make cultures such as the Chambri relevant to our own, she described non-Western personality configurations of men and women as permutations of established Western patterns (see Gewertz, 1984)[9]. In other words, in her concern to prove to American men and women that the social relationships they assumed to be inalterable were only a matter of custom and could be changed, she failed to take seriously enough the extent of cultural differences.

Although gender relationships among the Chambri are less directly applicable than Mead thought as models for Western men and women, the extent of the differences between their sociocultural system and our own can still be instructive. Because the Chambri system provides a distinctive contrast with our own, important aspects of our lives can be perceived with greater precision: through contrast with the cultural assumptions and social arrangements of a group such as the Chambri, our own set of assumptions and arrangements is thrown into relief. Moreover, by comparing not simply separate aspects of sociocultural systems but the systems themselves, we can see more clearly the nature of relationships between parts of a given system. More specifically, we can through

such comparisons work toward obtaining a more complete understanding of that which is contingent to, and that which is causative
of, particular gender definitions and relationships, including those
which we encounter in our own lives.

Thus, to the extent that we can through these comparisons
comprehend our own sociocultural system more fully, we should be
better able to formulate and appraise the possibilities for change in
our own lives. (For examples of recent cross-cultural comparisons
which contribute to the understanding of our own system, see
Etienne and Leacock, 1980; Rosaldo, 1980a; Ortner and
Whitehead, 1981; Strathern, 1981; Sacks, 1982; and Bell, 1983. See
also Marcus and Fischer, 1986, for an excellent discussion of the
nature and objectives of such comparisons.)

Although we disagree with Mead about the nature of the relations
between Chambri men and women – we will, in fact, argue that
neither dominates the other – and what we in our own culture can
learn from them, we are in full accord with her statement concerning
the sense of social responsibility which should inform research:

Our obligations in the choice of hypotheses about mankind are deep and
binding. As scientists pledged to search for the best hypotheses, we have
certain clear obligations. As members of human society ... we also have
clear obligations to explore actively those hypotheses which would seem to
open up the next important fields of research. (1949: 394)

When Mead wrote this passage she was concerned that her
research about constitutional types would be misconstrued as a
defense of racism. And we are concerned that our re-analysis of the
Chambri material and our disagreement with Mead will be misconstrued as support for those who argue that male dominance is
biologically determined and therefore inevitable. We wish to make
clear at the outset of this book that, although we believe Mead was
wrong about the Chambri, we believe her perspective that gender
relationships are, in primary measure, sociocultural constructs is
the only reasonable one.[10]

Her primary error in interpreting the Chambri, we argue, results
from her failure to follow far enough her own anthropological
perspective that cultural differences may indeed be so substantial as
to create very different sorts of persons than those existing in the
West. Significantly, it is precisely the opposite criticism – that she
overstated the extent of cultural differences – which has emerged in
the recent, widespread discussion of Mead's work (provoked by the

publication of Derek Freeman's (1983) *Margaret Mead and Samoa: The Making and Unmaking of an Anthropological Myth*), as the following passage from *Time* magazine indicates:

Coming of Age in Samoa, like much of Mead's work, attracted a wide audience for it implied criticism of Western civilization. The book said, in effect: The West features fidelity, competition, overheated sexual arrangements, a tight nuclear family, guilt, stress and adolescent turmoil; yet here are alleged primitives leading graceful lives of cooperation, adolescent bliss, casual family ties and easy sex, all without any signs of guilt or neurosis.

... Mead became the natural ally of those who promoted free education, relaxed sexual norms and green-light parenting ... Says Manhattan Psychologist Otto Klineberg: "She had a very definite influence in shaping public opinion, similar to that of Dr Spock. Mead and Spock reduced the emphasis on the biological side of childhood and adolescence and changed the pattern of child-rearing."

... Mead succeeded in swaying the minds of liberal educators and psychologists mostly by *dramatic but mistaken references to primitive living* [our emphasis] ... After Freeman's book, *Coming of Age in Samoa* may be increasingly regarded as a curious artifact from an ancient war (Leo, 1983: 52)

Although our position is that Mead underestimated the extent to which cultures differ from each other, this article criticizes her for exaggerating the extent of those differences. It asserts that she was wrong in suggesting that we in the West could learn from non-Western peoples about the existence of fundamental cultural alternatives. We were mistaken to have believed that her account of their lives could teach us that significant variability was possible with respect to child rearing, cooperation, or flexibility of family roles.[11] Our social arrangements thus receive confirmation because they are in general accord with a universal human pattern. Moreover, the ways in which our sociocultural system does differ from others give it an additional validity. This is a lesson we are supposed to learn from the article, and from the cartoon chosen to illustrate it. (See Cartoon 1, p. 10.) All we can learn from non-Western peoples, in other words, is that it is boring to be one of them.

Although the ethnocentrism of this *Time* magazine article is obvious, defending not only as inevitable but as superior what one might call "the American way," it may not be immediately clear that it is also reactionary. It seems to us that if the study of non-Western peoples demonstrates that no real cultural alternatives

"You have no idea what a drag it is, living in this god-
forsaken place, waiting for anthro-
pologists to turn up."

Cartoon 1.

exist, then significant sociocultural change is virtually out of the
question.[12] This implication is particularly frightening to Western
feminists who have worked to transform the world in which they
live. The article implies that if these social activists have been
successful at all, it has been at the tremendous cost of flouting that
which is naturally human – that which is universally true: namely,
those values held as axiomatic by Western males of a generation
ago.[13]

The 1,500 Chambri are from three villages located south of the
Sepik River on an island-mountain in Chambri Lake. Their socio-

cultural system has developed in complex interaction with those of their neighbors of the Middle Sepik. All were sedentary, occupying a variety of environments and exchanging their surpluses in a regional socioeconomic system. The Chambri supplied fish to the Sepik Hills peoples and the Iatmul supplied fish to the Sawos, receiving sago in return. The Chambri obtained shell valuables from the Iatmul by providing them with specialized Chambri products of stone tools and mosquito bags: the former were made by men and the latter by women. The Iatmul traded a portion of these Chambri products to the Sawos for shell valuables which both they and the Chambri used in their systems of affinal exchange.

The nature of this regional dependency shaped the development of each of these groups. In particular, the Chambri have been eager to borrow art and ceremonial forms from the Iatmul whose military and economic power impressed and, to some extent, regulated them. This Iatmul regulation was, we believe, of particular importance in shaping male-female relationships within the Chambri villages: because the Chambri supplied the Iatmul with important, specialized trade goods, they lived in relative peace, largely safe from Iatmul attack, and never developed a male-oriented military organization comparable in form to that of the Iatmul. Moreover, Chambri access to shell valuables was substantially dependent on the availability of these to their trading partners among the Iatmul. Consequently, Chambri men could not appreciably increase the flow of shells to them by increasing their production of items of trade. Thus the control of women and their products – mosquito bags in particular – was irrelevant to either the military or political viability of Chambri men. (See Weiner, 1976 and Etienne, 1980 for discussions of comparable circumstances in which the surplus production of women was not subject to male appropriation.)

The introduction of European steel tools and cloth mosquito nets destroyed the market for Chambri products and transformed the relationship between the Chambri and the Iatmul. Fighting between the two became increasingly frequent until around 1905, when the Chambri fled their island rather than risk further military encounters with Iatmul, whose ferocity had been augmented by the acquisition of a shotgun. Not until 1927, after the Australians had pacified the Iatmul, did the Chambri return to their island. Soon afterward, they began to participate extensively in labor migration and a cash economy.

However, these changes stemming from European influence

appear to have had surprisingly little effect on relationships between Chambri men and women. (See Weiner, 1980, for a similar observation.) Indeed, if anything, control of women had become even less relevant to male interests since the spheres of men and women had become further separated. While the women continued the subsistence trading of fish for sago, the men now increasingly devoted their energies to wage labor in order to acquire the money which was coming to displace shell valuables in their ceremonial exchanges. Thus, this pattern of interaction in which the control of women and their products is largely irrelevant to the political viability of Chambri men seems to have persisted from pre-contact times until the present. (However, as we will also discuss, the fact that money, since the late 1970s, no longer operates solely as the functional equivalent of shell valuables may soon come to create inequality between men and women.)

The Chambri encountered first by Mead and Fortune and then by us should therefore be understood as the product of a complex history of ecosystemic constraint and socioeconomic interaction. These processes – both prior and subsequent to contact – have already been discussed and analyzed in considerable detail by Deborah in *Sepik River Societies: A Historical Ethnography of the Chambri and their Neighbors* (1983). We will focus here on those cultural premises which have, we argue, shaped the perceptions, and thus compelled the actions of Chambri men and women within their regional socioeconomic system.

These cultural premises are by their nature embedded in Chambri lives: in Chambri political confrontations, intrigues, debates over sorcery; in their self descriptions, love letters, marriages, funerals; in their architecture, ritual paraphernalia, system of names; and in their myths, songs, dances. We find in these the evidence of their cultural assumptions. By confronting such a diversity of material and by alternating between data and interpretation we can both infer and test our ideas about the nature of the fundamental assumptions Chambri employ as they encounter each other and orient themselves in their world. In particular, we shall in this way derive Chambri ideas about the interests and strategies of men and women as well as demonstrate the significance of these ideas as they determine their actions and reactions.

Our most general perspective is, thus, that these cultural premises – rooted in a regional socioeconomic context – are employed by social actors to define themselves and their social objectivities. Although we recognize that there is substantial anthropological debate (see, for example, Shweder and Levine, 1984) as to whether an individual, in fact, experiences his or her own "self" and that of others in ways which are *fully* commensurate with premises of his or her culture about the nature of human beings – the nature of "persons" – nonetheless, it seems to us that most agree (see, for example, White and Kirkpatrick, 1985) that these premises do have a decisive role in shaping such experience.[14]

Certainly we will argue that the premises on which Chambri individuals base their sense of self are indeed comparable to those on which the Chambri cultural definition of person is based. Moreover, since these premises are the cultural categories of understanding through which Chambri formulate and interpret not only their experience and objectives but the experience and objectives of others, they also, in our view, provide the key for understanding much of Chambri social action.[15]

In Part One, we present the distinctively non-Western cultural premises about human beings, their objectives and their relationships which are shared by both Chambri men and women, but which are encountered and experienced differently by members of each group. In Part Two, we will then show the way that these cultural premises are embodied in social action. These two parts constitute a discussion regarding the culturally defined interests of Chambri men and women and the particular strategies members of each group employ in pursuit of their interests.

As we shall see, the strategies of men and women are sufficiently different so that, in most cases, men and women are able to pursue their separate concerns without domination by, or even interference from, members of the other group. In pursuing their concerns, men are plunged into perpetual competition with other men in which each seeks to achieve worth both by demonstrating the extent of his existing power and by augmenting his power from that of other men. The realm of male activity is, thus, characterized by a considerable elaboration of strategy and political form as each man attempts to succeed at the expense of the others. In contrast, because women are able to achieve worth in a more reliable and less competitive fashion, their strategies are relatively straightforward and can be independently pursued in a less complex social context. In order, therefore, to provide a complete portrayal of Chambri gender relationships, we must necessarily devote somewhat more space to the discussion of the strategies of men than of women.

In our Conclusion, we pursue Mead's concern that anthropology provide ideas about what our cultural alternatives might be at a difficult period in our own history. It was, after all, only a generation ago that many of our mothers, reading Margaret Mead's *Male and Female*, became convinced that anatomy was not, necessarily, destiny. Will our children be able to come of age with as great an expectation?

Part one

Cultural premises

Chapter 1
Entropy and the nature of indebtedness

Chambri men and women experience the world through a set of non-Western cultural premises concerning the nature of indebtedness and the nature of power. The primary debt is for physical and social existence itself: individuals are indebted to those who have engendered them and to those who have lost ancestral power to give them viability and social position. Men and women encounter indebtedness in different ways and their respective experiences of indebtedness lead them to employ different strategies to repay their debts.

A principal relationship of indebtedness between males exists between groups of wife-takers and wife-givers. Indeed, male political activity focuses on the struggle by men to pay their affinal debts to those who have provided their lives by providing their mothers. In their effort to be relatively successful in paying these debts, men are plunged into a competition for power. As we will see, power for the Chambri rests on an individual's capacity to use knowledge of secret names in order to identify with – indeed, incarnate – powerful lineage ancestors. The capacity to embody ancestral power becomes the basis of male identity and worth for this power is, in turn, the basis of ability to pay affinal and other debts as well as to shape social relationships more generally.

Wapiyeri's concern

Near the end of Deborah's first field trip in 1975, Wapiyeri, an old man who had been appointed as the leader – *Luluai* – of Indingai Village by the Europeans in the late 1930s,[1] called her to his house. He wished, he said, to tell her a myth. This was, itself, an unusual event, for Chambri rarely tell myths in so formal a manner.

17

Typically, myths are volunteered to explain those aspects of their lives which happen to be under discussion.[2] Moreover, Wapiyeri, as a respected and dignified Chambri, was among the least likely to ask Deborah the favor of a visit. Although he had always been gracious when she came to his large, rambling house to speak with him and his three wives, he had never before sought her company.

Wapiyeri probably had decided to tell Deborah this myth because he wished to enlist her services. When she was leaving his house, he handed her a letter which she was to deliver to his four sons in the capital city of Port Moresby, and gave her specific instructions to make sure that they returned home to Chambri as the letter directed. The letter was written for him by his youngest mission-educated son, David Wapi, who had acted as Deborah's research assistant during the previous year. David was the only one of his sons at home, and Wapiyeri very much needed the others to return from their sojourn as migrant laborers to fulfill their affinal obligations. He must have thought it fitting that Deborah bear this message to his sons because from his perspective she was, as a European, responsible in large measure for the transformation of the world that had resulted in their long-term absence.[3] The myth he told her that day was an argument, itself cast in traditional form, for the status quo; it was, we think, meant to convince her that his position was valid, so that she would be an effective advocate of his views when talking to his sons in the city.[4]

If Wapiyeri's sons chose to remain in Port Moresby, the consequence would be the end of his family as a political force. Sekumbumeri, his formerly large and powerful patriclan, had become stripped of its effective constituents by age, death, and labor migration: Wapiyeri was old; his brothers, dead; his sons, away and seemingly indifferent to his plight. If they could be induced to return home and recompense their affines – using the money which he thought they must have saved from their wages – then his clan would again become a strong and significant component of Indingai Village and of Chambri life in general.

In 1975, Sekumbumeri was one of, what were then, 34 patriclans – ranging in size from 10 to 79 members – within the three Chambri villages. A clan is a land-owning, residential and ceremonial group, referred to by the Chambri as "the people with the same totems." Although patriclan members claim descent from their patriclan founder, they do not keep extensive genealogies, and it is, instead, the eligibility to inherit access to a corpus of totemic names, both esoteric and exoteric, that links them together.

These names are totemic, for they refer both to the ancestors who once held them and to the portion of the natural realm – objects, territories, species and processes – owned and controlled by these ancestors. Correct utterance of these totemic names, particularly those which are esoteric, enables a man to establish an identification with his ancestors in which he incorporates their totemic power. With this power, the totemic operator can not only control the ancestral portion of the natural world but, in addition, can decisively shape social relations.[5]

Although these names are regarded as clan property and should be exercised on behalf of the clan, it is important to note that there is considerable competition among male agnates to gain access to these names and consequent power. The most successful in this competition is able to assume leadership over the clan through demonstrating control over a wide range of social relations, both internal and external to the clan. Conversely, the degree to which these social relations appear regulated – including the extent to which a leader can protect his clansmen from such dangers as attacks of sorcery – provides a measure of his power, and hence, of his esoteric knowledge.

Under the direction of such a leader, a clan assumes responsibility for payment of the bride-prices and subsequent affinal debts of each of its members; conversely, the bride-prices and later affinal presentations owed its members are paid to the clan as a collectivity. (As we will see, however, just as there is likely to be conflict within a clan concerning access to esoteric totemic names, there may be conflict over the distribution of these payments.) Affinal transactions are a major part of any ceremony a clan stages, and are particularly important at ceremonies of marriage, birth, initiation, and death. During these ceremonies, clan members celebrate the importance of their clan with long recitatives of their exoteric totemic names. Frequently, their chants also recount the travels of the clan's founder, often incarnate as a *masalai* (spirit) crocodile, swimming through clan-owned water and resting on clan-owned land. Their chanting often extends over several days and nights and, while they rest, their affines present their own recitatives in their turn.

The myth Wapiyeri told Deborah, which we have titled *The Marriages of Mandonk's Sisters*, follows. Mandonk is one of the totemic names of a crocodile spirit of Wapiyeri's clan and this story of Mandonk's affinal relationships, we will argue, pertains directly to Wapiyeri's own affinal preoccupation.

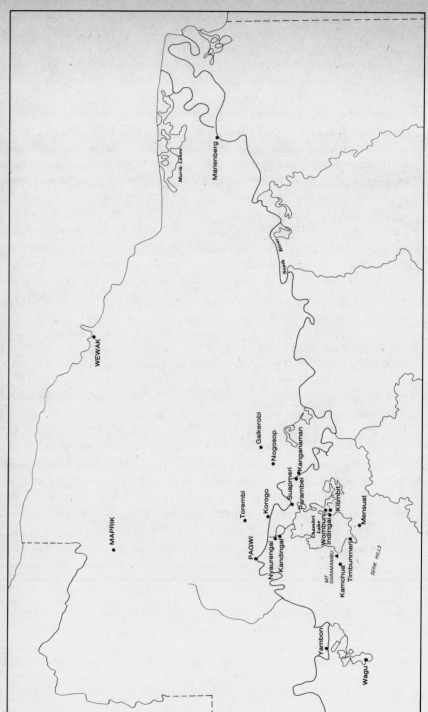

Map 2. Places mentioned throughout book

The marriages of Mandonk's sisters

Mandonk, the *masalai* crocodile, left his two sisters on Chambri Island when he went across the lake to Mt Garamambu. [See Map 2 for the location of places mentioned throughout this book.] The sisters, deciding to prepare sago, were at the grove of sago palms near the village of Kilimbit when they realized they had forgotten to bring with them the necessary coconut bast sieve.

Returning home for this, the sisters found an old woman cooking soup in their house. The old woman told them that she had been sent by Mandonk to take care of them. But she was lying. In fact, she was an *uncheban* [a non-totemic spirit] dressed in a grass skirt as a woman.[6] This *uncheban* had spilled his semen into the soup he was cooking. Suragwe, the younger of the two girls, suspected something was amiss, and fled the house to find her brother, who rose to the surface of Chambri Lake in a whirlpool to retrieve her. Yaproagwe, the elder sister, thought Suragwe foolish and gladly ate the soup that the *uncheban* had prepared. Soon she found herself pregnant and then understood that she had become the wife of the *uncheban*.

Soon after his son was born, the *uncheban* decided to go hunting. He killed two wild pigs and a bandicoot – so much meat that he could not carry it all. Bringing the bandicoot home with him, he asked Yaproagwe to prepare a soup with it while he returned to the bush to fetch the pigs.

First Yaproagwe broke her sons's fingers. Then she broke his wrist. But he did not die until she snapped his neck. "Good," she thought, "now I will cook a soup." Extracting all but his fingers from the soup, Yaproagwe placed her son's cooked body and some fried sago into a palm-bark basket. She then changed a small piece of wood into a radio transmitter by reciting her totemic names over it. She hung the enchanted wood underneath the floor of her house, near the area where her mosquito net hung. Finally, she filled her canoe with betel nuts, with betel pepper catkins and with coconuts, destroyed all of the other canoes, and set off to join her brother and sister at Garamambu.

When the *uncheban* came home with the dead wild pigs, his wife was nowhere in sight. He called her name, and the enchanted piece of wood answered: "Your son and I are sick. We are sleeping in the mosquito net. If you are hungry, eat the soup I have cooked." The *uncheban* began to eat, and soon came upon his son's fingers. "What's this," he thought, "bandicoots don't have fingers." The enchanted piece of wood told him to eat the meat and sago that he would find in the palm-bark basket. When he looked inside of it, he discovered the body of his son, and learned what his wife had done.

He decided to pursue and kill her, but found that she had broken all of the canoes. So, fastening one together with rope, and using a palm frond as a paddle, he set out across the lake to Garamambu.

Mandonk, meanwhile, had received his sister and, anticipating the *uncheban's* attack, brought all of the other *masalai* crocodiles together in his men's house. When the *uncheban* arrived, they were ready for him. Together they finished him off.

Suragwe did not think her brother should have welcomed Yaproagwe back home, for she, as the wife of an *uncheban*, was dirty. Mandonk listened to Suragwe and gave Yaproagwe a house far from all of the others, near the bush.

Yaproagwe was unhappy. She cried that her brother was not treating her well. She stayed all by herself, with no company except for Suragwe's daughter, who came to visit her from time-to-time. She was alone, and occupied herself by weaving fish baskets.

One day, when Yaproagwe was washing herself in a rivulet, she noticed that fish were pouring from her skin. The water around her had become full of them. She brought them home, smoked them, and soon her house was completely black from the smoke necessary to prepare all the fish she had produced. Her entire house was filled with fish, turtles, clams and snails – with all the good things from the water. With no more baskets to store them in, she asked her niece to bring her the sago palm leafstalks she needed to make new ones.

Now Yakosinmali, the sun, was in the habit of descending from his home in the sky every night to patrol the earth. One night, his son asked to be taken along and taught the custom of patrolling. The two of them descended to the earth on a ladder made of rattan. When it was almost daybreak, the young sun was nowhere to be found and his father had to ascend to the sky without him.

Finding himself alone on the earth, the young boy hid under the root of an ironwood tree, near the place where Yaproagwe bathed to produce her fish. Coming in the morning, as usual, Yaproagwe saw a luminescence pour from under the root of the ironwood tree. Thinking that she had found a *masalai*, Yaproagwe was relieved when the sun's boy explained himself. He asked to be left where he was until his father could come to find him that night, but Yaproagwe refused his request because she said that he would starve if left alone. She put him in a fish basket and carried him home. Since he gave off light, she hid him well by surrounding the basket in which she had placed him with the other old and smokey ones.

Meanwhile, the sun was searching for his child. Every night he would descend to the earth to look for him, but could not find him. And every morning he would ascend to the sky to tell his wife of his failure.

One day Suragwe and her daughter were out walking. While passing Yaproagwe's house, Suragwe thought to cook some food and called out to her sister for an ember. Yaproagwe, however, was out producing fish, and so Suragwe entered the house to get the fire. Surprised to see the house filled with all the good things from the water, Suragwe was reaching for the fire when a piece of rattan fell from a shelf into the fish basket where the young man was hidden. Opening the basket wider to extract the rattan,

Suragwe found the sun's boy, whose light came pouring forth. Suragwe climbed into the fish basket and had intercourse with him.

Yaproagwe came home to find them, and said: "Why have you come? Don't you remember that I smell – that I'm a dirty woman who was an *uncheban's* wife?"

"I came to get fire, but now I want to live here forever. Don't worry about the past. I'll help you work. I see you have brought fish home. Let me cook them for you."

"Get out of here. You never came to see me before."

Suragwe left, but returned with all of her belongings. Soon both sisters were pregnant by the sun's boy. And soon both delivered, Yaproagwe a boy and Suragwe a girl.

The sun's boy said: "It's been a year, and now it's time for my father to find me."

That night when he went out, his father found him. He brought his father to his house and told his story. After hearing the story, Yakosinmali, the sun, walked through the village, changing all the thatch of the houses into metal roofing with reflected rays. This he gave to Mandonk as bride-price for his sisters.

Everyone then went up to the sky to celebrate. After the party, Mandonk and his family returned to their houses. Yakosinmali, his son, his daughters-in-law and his grandchildren all stayed in the sky.

The myth seems to be composed of three episodes which we think of as follows: Yaproagwe Weds the *Uncheban*, Yaproagwe Stands Alone, and finally, The Sisters Marry. Each expresses a different aspect of the male preoccupation with affinal indebtedness and, collectively, they explore the kinds of relationships which may be engendered by alternative forms of marriage and, indeed, by an alternative to marriage itself.[7] Since affinal relationships are the principal arena in Chambri society for the expression of political concerns – for the expression of power – this myth is exploring a subject of fundamental importance to the Chambri.

The first episode introduces the characters and the relationships which exist between them. Mandonk, Yaproagwe and Suragwe are all, as siblings, members of the same patriclan. Since Mandonk, as elder brother, is in charge of his sisters, neither sister is surprised to learn that he has delegated an old woman to look after them while he is away – although Suragwe, to be sure, has doubts about the actual identity of the old woman. The sisters, moreover, as unmarried women, are responsible for preparing food such as sago for themselves and for their brother.

The trouble begins, of course, with Yaproagwe's naivete. As elder sister, she should have known more about the world than did Suragwe, yet it is she who is tricked into drinking the semen of the devious *uncheban*. That she becomes pregnant through drinking the semen is a further indication that matters are going awry, since even in their myths, the Chambri mark the differences between stomachs and wombs.[8]

The irregularity of the conception and gestation of this child is mirrored in his irregular – indeed, entirely peripheral – social position. If normal biological and social processes had prevailed, the child would have been born into a network of matrilateral and agnatic kin: Mandonk would be his *wau*, his mother's brother, and the lineages of both of his parents would have been brought into close relationship. But Mandonk was never paid bride-price for his sister; the *uncheban* is without agnates. The child, therefore, has only the *uncheban* and Yaproagwe as kin and thus lacks full social reality.[9]

The *uncheban* has behaved autocosmically rather than socially: he spills his semen into a soup and then consumes a soup made of the child of this emission. His anomalous child, the product of his masturbation, dies and is then reabsorbed into its genitor because the *uncheban* activated no social processes while conceiving it. That Yaproagwe dispatches this child is not tragedy nor even tragic: rather than presenting a view of humanity or of the human condition, this episode is, instead, a demonstration of the social prerequisites of life in Chambri society.

In contrast to the first episode of the story where the *uncheban* is socially disengaged by his own choice, the second episode indicates that Yaproagwe is socially disengaged by the choice of others. She has returned to her family but is ostracized by them. Told that she is dirty, she is given a house near the bush where she lives closer to animals than to humans. There she becomes, from the Chambri perspective, like those animals, a source of extraordinary fecundity. Fish pour from her skin, and soon her entire house is full with all of the good things from the water – including the clams and snails whose shells, the *kina* and *talimbun*, are used by the Chambri as the valuables for bride-prices.[10] Before, as the wife of the *uncheban*, she had a husband but no bride-price; subsequently, while living alone close to the animals, she has bride-price but no husband. Before, when she was tricked by a non-social male into drinking the semen soup, she produced a human who lacked social reality; subsequently, when living by herself apart from humans she can only parthenogenetically reproduce fish.

She is not, however, an animal, regardless of how closely she resembles one, because she remains committed to the cultural transformation of the products of her body by smoking the fish she produces (see Levi-Strauss, 1969). Nor is her social isolation complete since her niece visits her and supplies her with sago palm leafstalks to make the baskets needed to contain her harvest.

Moreover, in the third episode of the story, she discovers Yakosinmali's son. The sun's boy belongs to a powerful lineage, and his father, Yakosinmali, is entirely willing to pay Mandonk bride-price for both the sisters. His bride-price is, indeed, particularly generous since it consists of corrugated metal roofs which only one as wealthy as a European could give. These corrugated metal roofs which cover the houses of the village literally and figuratively reflect the power of the sun and give notice to all that those who have become indebted to Mandonk and his agnates are important affines. Mandonk can, in addition, expect periodically to receive affinal recompense from Yakosinmali throughout the life cycles of the children of Yaproagwe and Suragwe. Appropriately this time, conception is normal, through womb rather than through stomach.

The myth presents the overall conclusion that women must be married and that it is essential that they marry the right sort of men, those who accept relationships of indebtedness to their affines.[11] Those who contemplate dispensing with affinal obligations would be like the *uncheban* who is not only ultimately unsuccessful in his efforts to acquire a wife but who is profoundly non-human. Indeed, the second episode of the myth suggests that unless a woman is fully engaged in the social forms which constitute proper marriage, her reproduction – both in its manner and in its product – will be fundamentally non-human. The myth thus makes clear that *because* these alternatives to a proper marriage are asocial, they lack validity.

This conclusion is not entirely a reflection of a simple moralism – an indigenous functionalism – that has individuals necessarily defining their self-interests as consonant with social need, but rather reflects, as we shall see in detail in the next chapter, the Chambri assumption that the only way in which individuals can establish themselves as persons at all is through a set of social relationships.[12] Neither men nor women nor their offspring, this myth concludes, can as autocosms achieve viability. Although social life is characterized by relationships in which autonomy is curtailed through indebtedness and other entanglements, it is, nonetheless, just these relationships which bestow human existence itself.

The political significance of affinal indebtedness

From the Chambri perspective, Yakosinmali as a wife-taker would be considered indebted, and hence inferior, to Mandonk as a wife-giver. Chambri wife-takers are regarded as owing their lives to those who have provided them with their mothers, who are the sources of nurture and life. Bride-price and subsequent affinal presentations are the means by which payment is made on these debts, the means by which the members of a patriclan purchase from their matrilateral kinsmen the essential rights to control themselves and their children. Thus, jural membership in Chambri patriclans is contingent upon the payment of debts to affines.

However, despite repeated payments, affinal debts can never be fully settled.[13] The primary reason for this rests in a cultural assumption that those who have caused life remain more important than those whose lives they have caused. No man – or, to be more accurate, no clan – can hope to fulfill affinal obligations completely, no matter how generous the response. Indeed, the perpetuation of affinal indebtedness is implicit in the very way affinal payments must be made. The fundamental inequality between wife-givers and wife-takers is reflected in the cultural requirement that the exchanges between them be conducted through items of incommensurate nature (see Forge, 1972: 537). Valuables move in one direction and women, food, and other representations of nurture move in the other. The incommensurability of that which is exchanged denotes and perpetuates the inequality between the two groups linked through these exchanges.

Inequalities between affines become translated into inequalities between other non-related groups. Although the Chambri consider individuals and groups that are not linked through marriage as potentially equal, differences in relative power and prestige – in political status – can be established and maintained between groups of men when those that are "more than equal" assist their "less than equal" neighbors to meet their affinal debts. When a Chambri and the members of his clan cannot amass sufficient valuables to compensate wife-givers in a creditable manner, they will seek assistance from an unrelated clan. This clan, in return for its assistance, gains control over its client – over its land and water rights, its totemic names and powers and other valuables – until the debt can be repaid by the client clan either by itself or on its behalf, by yet another clan. In the latter and more frequent case, the client clan may simply have found another patron. Indeed, wealthy clans compete with each other to acquire new clients, either from those clans recently distressed by their obligations or from those which have already become clients of other clans.

The inequality inherent in affinal exchange ensures that no clan will be politically ascendant over all of the others. However, as the system works out in practice, this inequality ramifies as the affinal relations of some provide others with the opportunity to prove themselves ascendant not only over their clients but over other only moderately wealthy groups which have been able to acquire fewer clients.

It is with reference to the unequal relationships established between groups of men through their marriages that Wapiyeri's concern that his sons come home and recompense their affines must be understood. Three of Wapiyeri's four migrant sons had married Chambri women before they left their village. They were not, however, maintaining their affinal presentations to their wife-givers. Even with the help of his one resident son, David, who had some income as Deborah's research assistant, Wapiyeri was unable to cover all of the obligations which had been incurred by his sons. Patronage of Sekumbumeri was inevitable, unless the four migrants returned home to assume their responsibilities.[14]

Thus Wapiyeri's concern over the fate of Sekumbumeri was reflected in the myth he told Deborah as he sought to enlist her help in effecting the return of his sons. *The Marriages of Mandonk's Sisters* shows clearly the preoccupation of Chambri men with what might be called the "politics of affinal exchange." This preoccupation was also recognized by Margaret Mead who wrote:

Once one has obtained [property], it becomes a counter in the games that men play; it is no longer concerned with the underlying economics of life, but rather with showing one's appreciation of one's brother-in-law, soothing someone's wounded feelings, behaving very handsomely when a sister's son falls down in one's presence. The minor war-and-peace that goes on all the time among the men, the feelings that are hurt and must be assuaged, are supported by the labour and contributions of the women. (1935: 254)

Mead is correct in her description of the way Chambri men use property: they are indeed preoccupied with maintaining appropriate relationships between wife-givers and wife-takers. Mead was wrong, however, to suggest that the "war-and-peace" that goes on among the men is minor and just an unimportant matter of hurt feelings. Political viability is, after all, at stake if sufficient property cannot be acquired by the members of a patriclan to enable them to show adequate "appreciation of one's brother-in-law." That some clans will lose their viability is, indeed, entirely predictable, given Chambri assumptions about the nature of entropy.[15]

The dissipation of power

When we arrived on Chambri Island in late 1983, we inquired after Wapiyeri and his clan. He was dead, we were told. His sons had failed to return and his clan had been absorbed.[16] We then asked Patrick Yarapat, a man who had been one of Wapiyeri's principal rivals, why Wapiyeri and his once strong clan had entirely lost their power and, thus, their autonomous identity. Yarapat's answer focused on the five sticks Wapiyeri had kept leaning against the wall in his house.

Kalambunsui was the first man who held the power of everything. He made power happen. He gave most of his power to Mariwansik. Mariwansik belongs to Wombun Village. Later, other men got some of the power. They are Yamko, a big ancestor of Wombun; Japawai of Wombun; Sandar of Indingai; Komario of Indingai; Kimbinmeri, a leader of Kilimbit. All of these men who had some of the power died at the same time that the grandfather of Wapiyeri died. The five sticks Wapiyeri had in his house were what was left of the power these men had.

Over time, the power created by Kalambansui became diffused and dispersed. Mariwansik inherited most, but not all of his power, passing on some of reduced power to Yamko, Japawai, Sandar, Komario, and Kimbinmeri. All that was left of this original and formerly concentrated power was contained in Wapiyeri's five sticks. And, as implied by the context in which this story was related, the residual power available to Wapiyeri proved insufficient to ensure the political autonomy of his clan. All clans are subject to this process of entropy, although as the change in the relative importance of clans also implies, some lose more power than others. It is as part of the relationship between generations that power is dispersed, dissipated and ultimately lost and that debt is created. Power is transmitted when a father, and to a lesser extent, mother's brother, attempt to ensure the viability of a boy by giving him totemic names which convey power. Later, as well, when he becomes an adult, he is given additional names and consequent powers, particularly by his father. However, men are reluctant to pass on their most powerful names even to their sons, and many of these names, the Chambri think, die with them.[17] In addition, those names the younger men do know may become ineffective if too many try to use them.[18] Since this transmission of power is limited and imperfect, male agnates of the senior generation are likely to be more powerful than those of the junior generation while, at the same time, the juniors are indebted to their seniors for those names they have received.

The Chambri assumption that the course of social life is characterized by entropy – that power diminishes with each generation – affects the efforts of Chambri men to pursue what is their fundamental objective: to become *at least* the equal of all other Chambri men.[19] Men seek equality not only as they make payments on their ontological debts to their seniors – both affines as well as agnates – but as they attempt to accumulate power comparable in amount to that of these senior men and others. Indeed, because of perpetual indebtedness to affines and because of entropy, the desire to be the equal of all others means that men always aspire to more power than they can ever obtain. Thus, the elusive goal of equality impels rather than restrains men in their competition to acquire power, generating yet further relations of inequality.[20]

Men will strive in the course of their lives to become the equals of their agnatic seniors by attempting to repay their debts as well as to accumulate power. Payment of debts to agnatic seniors (and in lesser extent to a mother's brother) generally takes the form of contributing energy and resources to their projects. Becoming the equal of agnatic seniors in power is more difficult. To achieve equality with agnatic seniors – among those favored by the process of entropy – yet to avoid direct and potentially dangerous confrontation with them, individuals strive to acquire power primarily from outside their clan. The competition is intense: since the pool of power is dwindling, each must strive for a disproportionate share in order to become equal to the important members of the senior generation. (Significantly, in this universe of male rivalry, one of the least competitive relationships is between mother's brother and sister's son. As we will show in Chapter 6, a man often achieves equality with his senior agnates only through receiving the essentially maternal support of food and nurture from his mother's brother.)

The principal arena where power may be both displayed and

acquired is that of affinal politics. Junior men begin to demonstrate their power relative to their agnatic seniors as they come to direct their clans in affinal exchanges. To the extent that they prove more successful than their seniors in these exchanges, they establish that they are no longer inferior to their seniors in power. In addition, as individuals achieve success in the leadership of their clans, they reduce the extent of their inequality to their affines. As we have seen, each Chambri man by the fact of his birth incurs an ontological debt, substantially greater than that owed to his senior agnates. Since wife-givers have provided life, wife-takers remain perpetually indebted to them, irrespective of the magnitude of their affinal payments; nonetheless, particular wife-takers can be relatively more successful than others in their efforts to pay their affinal debts. Moreover, their success in this realm is the basis for further acquisition of power: it is in the relative capacity to pay these debts that individuals and their clans not only achieve eminence but formally subsume the power of others.

Chambri men, thus, engage as patrons and clients in the politics of affinal exchange in order to attempt, in a world generally characterized by entropy, to display and acquire the power necessary to become as nearly as possible the equals of those who have caused them and, as well, of their peers.

Women also strive to achieve equality with their predecessors. Girls, too, are given names which give them viability. Since they receive fewer names than do their brothers, and certainly no names which confer political power, relatively little is lost on their behalf and consequently the debts they incur to their agnates are easily covered by their bride-prices. Chambri women also acquire major ontological debts by the fact of their births. However, because women can repay such debts and men cannot, this leads each to seek to establish equality in very different ways.

Through reproduction, women can replace those who gave them life and so entirely redeem themselves from ontological debt. Moreover, perhaps since women can validate themselves completely in this way, they do not measure their relative equality in terms of the accumulation of power. Thus, neither affinal competition nor the fact of entropy brings them into competition with each other as they pursue their strategies to achieve equality.

However, before we can discuss further the differential responses of men and of women to the preoccupying problem of achieving worth, we must first consider in more detail the Chambri concept of what people are thought to be.

Chapter 2
Names and personal identity

In Port Moresby, Wapiyeri's letter in hand, Deborah happened upon Andrew Kinsinkamboi, a man from Indingai Village who had been part of a small delegation of Chambri singers and dancers sent to perform there at the National Cultural Festival.[1] Despite visits to Rabaul and Madang as a young man some 15 years earlier, Kinsinkamboi had never before been to a city as large and bustling as Port Moresby had become. When Deborah asked him how he was enjoying his time away from Indingai, he admitted that the sights impressed him, but the city and its people made him anxious because "no one here knows my names."

In the context of our discussion of Chambri preoccupations with achieving equality, we indicated that clan power is ultimately augmented or depleted through the politics of affinal exchange. However, the outcome of this political process is regarded by the Chambri as the culmination of prior transactions in which individuals – such as Kinsinkamboi – experience anxiety or elation as their social identities are depleted or enhanced through the loss or acquisition of totemic names. Individual Chambri, during the course of daily life, experience shifts in their reputations as they have or do not have the names which convey power; and this is well before their clans become clients or patrons.

Each Chambri is given totemic names by his or her patrilineal and matrilateral relatives. Men acquire more of these names, as well as names which are more powerful, than do women. Both men and women receive more, as well as more powerful names, from their patrilineal than from matrilateral kin. Nonetheless, all Chambri derive much of their initial identity through their possession of these totemic names. They become in substantial measure the incarnation of their patrilineal and matrilateral relationships.[2]

31

These names both reflect and affect the transactions which constitute a person's fundamental social relationships and identity. (See Mauss, 1969, for a comparable view.) Names which are public knowledge may be used as terms of address. They may be the basis of claims to use particular resources: someone, for instance, may assert the right to use a stand of sago palms because it is regarded as under the control of the ancestor whose name s/he carries. In addition, these publicly known totemic names confer some measure of ancestral protection against the hazards of life, including the minor malevolence of others.

Names which are secret provide a man, in particular, with a much more significant part of his identity – his reputation for having power. Secret names, when used effectively, enable a man to establish identity with his ancestors and to become the embodiment of their power. That a man is powerful, thus necessarily indicates that he possesses powerful totemic names. These names must remain secret or, the Chambri think, their power will be alienated or diluted through use by others. (See Barth, 1975; Harrison, 1982; and Jorgensen, n.d. for similar discussions concerning the relationship between ritual power and secrecy.)

However, as long as a man is recognized as having power by virtue of his success in maintaining his network of social relationships, no one is likely to risk his retribution by attempting to discover or to use his secret names, nor is he likely to be so insufficiently vigilant as to reveal them. Conversely, if an individual suffers misfortune in his social relationships – for example, when Wapiyeri's sons refused to return home or when a death occurs, inevitably viewed as caused by sorcery – it may be thought that his capacity to use the totemic names which should confer power has become impaired. Something is amiss: others may have learned his secret names; others may have become strong enough to use these names without fear of retribution. Clansmen fear that if this process continues, they will, as a collectivity, eventually become so weakened that they must yield their remaining power and resources to a patron clan.[3]

Chambri, as can be seen, attribute all of the fortunes and misfortunes of social life to the efficacy of their totemic names. When a man knows or suspects that his social transactions are impaired, he consequently fears that his names have lost their power for him. As he experiences loss of power, he feels not only diminished in his identity but also threatened in his health. Both social identity and physical viability are regarded as direct manifestations of ancestral power.

Kinsinkamboi, while in Port Moresby, seems to have anticipated that misfortune would result from his experience of diminished identity. Because – a few other Chambri aside – no one there knew his public names, much less knew that he had secret names, his social context was too meager to give him much recognition and substantiation as a person.[4] Far from being able to augment his identity so that he could become more nearly the equal to those who had caused him, Kinsinkamboi may well have felt drained of his identity in these circumstances of social isolation. Moreover, it is under just these circumstances in which he had little control over his social relationships that he would be likely to doubt his capacity to sustain his physical viability.

From the Chambri perspective, his predicament was not serious because his social isolation was only temporary. Even if he became ill in Port Moresby he would be able to reconstitute himself on his return to Chambri.[5] The circumstances of those Chambri who disrupt their relationships at home are much more perilous. As the following case study shows, a loss of the crucial relations which sustain personal identity may, at the same time, indicate what the Chambri would interpret as a fatal impairment of a person's relationships with both living and dead.

The life and death of Francis Yaboli

Just before Deborah first arrived on Chambri Island in 1974, Francis Yaboli, a young man in his late twenties from Wombun Village, died after years of heavy drinking. According to the doctor who eventually attended him, his hemorrhaging came from drinking a bottle of methylated spirits. Since many Chambri have drunk methylated spirits without obvious ill effects, they assumed that Yaboli had been ensorcelled. The instrumental cause of his death they easily diagnosed as "Eagle Magic."[6]

The question which continued to interest the Chambri was who had actually invoked this magic. Indeed, men from all three Chambri villages convened repeatedly in one of the men's houses to address this question in formal debate. To better understand their preoccupation with this death, Deborah tried to find out from the debates and conversations as much as she could about Yaboli: what sort of man was he that he had provoked another to kill him?

Yaboli had recently eloped to the town of Wewak with Kermana, a woman from Indingai Village. This was a matter of note to the Chambri for several reasons. Because this marriage was between members of two largely endogamous villages, it was seen as affecting the collective interests of the members of both villages.[7] Consequently, many more individuals were scrutinizing this marriage than was usual. That this marriage was an elopement exacerbated feelings in this already uneasy situation. Moreover, this particular elopement evoked further disapproval because no bride-price was forthcoming. Kermana's three brothers, in particular, were made additionally angry because rumors came from Wewak that Yaboli often had severely beaten Kermana.

Affinal relationships were further strained by the intervention of two unrelated individuals, both drinking friends of Yaboli from the third Chambri village of Kilimbit. Yaboli apparently gave A$30.00 to Pekur, one of these friends, while they were on a binge in the town of Maprik.[8] On his return home, Pekur was to deliver this money to Kermana's brothers with the promise that an additional A$70.00 was soon to come as bride-price. However, Pekur decided to remain at Maprik and so passed on the money to Leo Konge, their other Chambri drinking friend. Konge did return home but Kermana's brothers never received the money. Moreover, Yaboli's agnates were furious that Pekur and Konge had concerned themselves in business not their own.

Finally, a distant agnate of Kermana and her brothers became involved. Apparently, David Massam had asked Yaboli to buy him a bottle of liquor while the two of them were at the Maprik Hotel. Yaboli had refused and Massam retaliated by threatening Yaboli's life. Massam wrote this threat down in a notebook, an action he later claimed was justified by reason of his kinship with Kermana. Furthermore, as her kinsman, he was representing her interests and those of her brothers by alerting Yaboli to the gravity of ignoring affinal debts. Kermana's brothers denied this explanation and refused to take any responsibility for Massam's actions.

Such was the information that provided the substance of Chambri discussion, both formal and informal. But, to Deborah, it did not immediately appear to answer the question of who Yaboli *actually* was: no one, for instance, had speculated as to why he had drunk so much and why he had beaten his wife. Even when Deborah pressed her inquiries, the only response she was given was that the reason he drank was that he was a drinker and the reason he beat his wife was because that was his custom. No one speaking either in or outside of the debates, even when prompted by the newly arrived anthropologist, reflected on what we might regard as the underlying reasons for his conduct. It became evident that Francis Yaboli was not to them a subjectivity, expressing discontent and alienation through anti-social behavior, to be understood as perhaps a novel consequence of his own formative experiences.

However, from the Chambri perspective, they were describing exactly who Yaboli, in fact, was: he was a man who drank and disrupted his social networks. And it was both obvious and significant to them that because his social transactions had become as they were he could no longer constitute himself as a viable person. In their view, he was as good as dead even before he actually decided to drink the bottle of spirits: the ineffectuality with which he attempted to conduct his social relationships testified to a critical loss of his power. His death was inevitable because he lacked sufficient strength to protect himself.

(We do recognize that much may be left tacit in ordinary cultural discourse. However, we consider it significant that we never heard Chambri discuss the causes of behavior, whether of their own or of others – either in response to our persistent questioning or in conversations with each other – through reference to an "underlying" subjectivity. Chambri do have emotion, intention and experience but they do not understand these as constituting themselves as subjectivities: that is, they do not see themselves as having an individually distinctive pattern of dispositions, capacities and perspectives. Nor do the Chambri ever refer to other characteristics which define a subjectivity such as the presence of a "character" or a "personality" in which the cluster of dispositions, capacities and perspectives is seen as internally integrated, having developed gradually over time as the result of "formative" experiences. Even individuals who behave in ways the Chambri consider to be insane (such as the young man who wanders aimlessly, and sometimes naked, throughout the three Chambri villages, sleeping outdoors without protection despite rain and mosquitos) are regarded as victims of sorcery, not as distraught because of some inner conflict. In these cases, as in Yaboli's instance, aberrant behavior is explained through reference to disrupted social relationships. In contrast, Americans, for instance, do frequently speculate about the reasons particular people act as they do by reference to individually distinctive patterns of dispositions, capacities, and perspectives.)[9]

No one during the debates expressed surprise that Yaboli had died; the discussion, instead, was concerned with who had acquired his power. Clearly power had shifted away from Yaboli and his clan and quite possibly the man who had attacked him was the one who had taken that power. The following excerpt from the debates reveals clearly the relationship Chambri posit between names, power, and persons.

Michael Kubusa (Kermana's eldest brother): Who calls my name that I am a magic man, he has to come before me with book and pen. He has to write down the kind of magic I sent to Francis Yaboli to make him die. Patrick Yarapat [an Indingai big man and rival to Kubusa], you call my name. I am very sorry but my father, Akaman, didn't teach me his names. He didn't have any magic at all, and so he didn't teach me his names. I think you just call my name because every morning and every afternoon I come to this men's house and beat the drum.[10] This is why you call me a magic man. What of the magic axe that Patrick Yarapat keeps in his house? That axe is not his. His father, Kanda, didn't have names for it. Kanda didn't have that magic axe before.[11] Please, I don't want anyone to call my name, to call me a magic man. When I was working in the Mission as a teacher, and going around the Sepik, I didn't learn any names or kill anyone from any other place through magic. I swear by God, I tell you all.

Ambunowi (Kermana's youngest brother): I am telling you people of the villages that you yourselves are spoiling everything. We, all the brothers of Kermana, we don't know that she even married Francis Yaboli. For Kermana's sake, don't say that we killed him through our magic. We are very sorry, but we have no magic names from our fathers. When you overhear these names coming from our mouths, then you can call us magic men. We don't know what David and Pekur did, what happened at the Maprik Hotel.

Patrick Yarapat (Kubusa's rival): All of us have to wait for the Council and for the police.[12] We don't know when they are coming. Please, I always tell you that you must keep your wits about you when you are drunk. A bottle of drink can spoil you. You can tell names and this can bring trouble from a robber of them. He can then use them against you. You know that I am a village leader. When I hear things, I let you know. We don't know who will go to prison over Francis Yaboli. But, this men's house is in the center of the village. When people are walking past, they can hear our secrets. When you talk about secret names, find a special place.

Wapiyeri (a rival of Yarapat): When our fathers were living on Chambri Island, they were really a magic people. They killed many men and women through their magic names.[13] But we, their sons, haven't one single name. But, there are some sons who do have these names. Before, when our fathers killed someone, they killed a pig to take away the bad spirit. Now, those who have the powers, they don't kill a pig, and we don't know who they are.

Edmund Maik (Francis' older brother): Massam wrote in a book that Francis will die. Thus, Francis died. Here is the book, and here are David's words. The words killed Francis, and Massam must go before the magistrate. That Francis married Kermana and no bride-price came, this is nothing. The words in the book did it all.[14]

The debates clearly were focused on who had the power to kill Francis Yaboli. Michael Kubusa and Ambunowi both reiterate that they were not magic men because they had not learned the proper names. Kubusa, moreover, addressed what he saw as a weakness in his defense. He was accused, he suggested, because "every morning and every afternoon I come to this men's house and beat the drum." Some might, therefore, know him as a traditionalist and expect him to have learned the appropriate magic names from Akaman, his father. He assured us that this was not the case because he had spent much of his life "in the Mission as a teacher, and going around the Sepik." Thus he was not at home to learn the names which would have allowed him to ensorcell Yaboli.

When Kubusa and Ambunowi asserted that they were people without magic names, everyone was aware that they were probably lying. Indeed, their behavior while denying that they had these powers was just the behavior which suggested that they did have them. By responding to accusations or by acting as though they were regarded as suspects, they presented themselves as men of power. They were, however, unwilling actually to admit that they are sorcerers because a confession would be the sort of evidence that could get them convicted of sorcery at the government court.[15] Moreover, a confession might provoke a concerted effort at revenge.

Chambri frequently think they know when people are lying, just as they usually think they know which persons possess knowledge of powerful secret names; nevertheless they are by no means invariably certain of what other people are up to or what the actual extent of their knowledge and power may be. Consequently, lies and bluffs are used to establish reputations for totemic power, reputations which then become further tested in the context of affinal exchange. What Chambri surmise about another becomes part of that person's social position and, hence, identity. But it does not, for them, point to any inner and defining subjectivity.

In Chambri society, thus, the distance between what we in the West would consider someone "really is" and his or her social relationships, including his or her status and roles, vanishes. A Chambri is regarded as what s/he does, what s/he has and, given the Chambri view of magic and totemic power, what s/he knows or is thought to know. The attributes which give individuals their identity as particular human beings are both manifested in and produced by their social relationships. Individuals are, therefore, regarded by the Chambri as, essentially, the embodiment of their particular social contexts.

But do individual Chambri see themselves as others see them? In other words, might Yaboli experience himself as a unique subjectivity – as a unique cluster of dispositions, capacities and perspectives – apart from his social position? We cannot, of course, be certain in his case. However, we do have available an autobiographical statement made by someone who was about his age, also a heavy drinker and one of his friends. Several months after Yaboli died, Deborah's 25-year-old research assistant, Joseph Kambukwat, came by her house and poured out this emotional and rather drunken explanation of himself and why, for fear of sorcery, he could no longer work for her.

The life of Joseph Kambukwat

My father died when I was young. He was fooling around with a woman from Timbunmeri, and the Timbuns ensorcelled him.[16] I was sleeping on his chest when he died. He bled from his mouth and died. I finished my apprenticeship at Technical College and worked for P.W.D. [Public Works Department], earning A$80.00 each fortnight.[17] They put A$30.00 away for me. My teacher was no good. I hit him with a piece of wood because he didn't tell me that there was a live electrical wire next to the beam I was working on. Then I joined the Police. I was only fifteen and could join because I had finished Form Two and was five feet two inches tall. In Moresby I earned only A$7.00 per fortnight, and had to buy all of my provisions. This was for eight months while training. Then came Rabaul, where I worked in an office because my superiors trusted me. The girl I met was paid A$100.00, but then I felt sorry for Bill Simbuk and gave her to him. He couldn't be loved until then, so I gave the girl her transportation and a radio and a tape recorder. These cost A$45.00 and A$30.00. I had plenty of fights there. The first one was with a European who touched the blouse of a native girl. He wanted to rape her and so I knocked all of his teeth out. He died in the hospital. I fought with a policeman too. There was a riot. The Tolais don't play around when they fight.[18] One policeman didn't care. He just stood around, and so I split his head open with a billy club. They fired me for this, and it went to the Supreme Court, where I paid A$30.00. Ken Dowry hired me to measure crocodile skins.[19] He paid me A$20.00 a fortnight, but he made more, so I quit this work. Then you came and now I don't want to look at you. People say you should have hired Yambumbe's family, and I don't want to talk anymore. But I will say that with Michael Somare and Independence, Papua New Guineans will no longer be behind Europeans.[20]

Even here, in Joseph Kambukwat's spontaneous attempt to explain himself – to make himself known and understood to Deborah – he revealed no subjectivity. He described none of the dispositions, capacities and perspectives which, for us, constitute the self: he did not view himself as having a unique character which had been formed by his particular experiences with both natives and Europeans. Instead, by his own account, he was the catalog of his transactions, be these of equality or inequality, be these commercial, social or violent. He was the person, to be more explicit, who was paid A$20.00 a fortnight to measure crocodile skins, who helped Bill Simbuk find a woman and who caused the death of a would-be rapist. In his effort to account for himself, he was not claiming that these transactions were reflections (or causes) of a unique set of inner and private dispositions, capacities and perspectives but rather, he was presenting himself as these transactions.

The cultural categories through which Joseph expressed his sense of self are, thus, comparable to those on which the Chambri definition of person is based: his identity to himself was defined in the same terms as was his identity to other Chambri.[21]

If, as we have argued, a Chambri is defined by his or her social context, his or her identity should be the product of the relationships which compose this context. As these relationships are augmented or diminished by his or her transactions, so too is his or her identity. And, as we have seen, these transactions and identity are regarded as affected by and embodied in the names s/he has. The relative degree of success of a Chambri leader, for instance, in establishing favorable relationships is seen by the Chambri as, in turn, coextensive with his knowledge of powerful totemic names. But a leader like Yarapat is qualitatively no different from his less successful neighbors – Kubusa, Ambunowi, Kambukwat or even Yaboli; he has no unique constellation of dispositions, capacities and perspectives which form him as a novel subjectivity but is, instead, more of what they are like. He has been more greatly augmented by his transactions than they have by theirs. Because of his powerful names, he has more nearly, more completely, become those who have caused him. Rather than seeking to differentiate themselves from their ancestors, Chambri aspire in important ways, through a process more of devolution than evolution or development, to become them.

Cultural assumptions and the misunderstanding of the Chambri

One of the major reasons, in our view, that Mead failed properly to understand the Chambri as persons – and thus misunderstood the relationship between Chambri men and women and the interests and strategies of each – is that she viewed them in terms of a culturally alien and Western model.[22] Following this model, she saw them as subjectivities which had developed as a result of emotionally formative experiences; she did not see them as repositories of social relationships. Chambri men and women, she thought, are different from American men and women: they have had different influences and these have produced different subjectivities. Consider, for example the methodology Mead devised while working among the Chambri between January and April, 1933.[23] The following document, which appears in her unpublished field notes and is entitled "Working Plan for Investigation of Personality Formation, March 20, 1933," nicely illustrates this Western view of persons:

Suggestion: That key to personality development and emotional tone is to be found in the organization of the women's groups and the relationship of children of both sexes to women rather than to men.

Points: Large size of informal women's group, continual aggregation of this group, association with constant eating, gay and sociable preparation of food, warmth of emotional tone between women, and the extension of this tone to children of both sexes under five or six, and to females for life.

Cross cousin marriage of the lien type assuring that a girl marries into a group of female kin who regard her as one of them, not as an intruder.

Preference for marrying women from the same group, so that women in a house and co-wives are all friends.

This eliminates conflict between mothers over children.

House boy [men's house] organization prevents any father-daughter relationship and so decrees that a girl suffers no social weaning trauma, either in childhood or at marriage.

Quantitate and check thus: Living or dead own mothers and the personality of living ones.

Relationship of father's other wives to own mother.

Relationship of elder brothers' wives and small papas' [father's younger brothers] wives to own mother.

Size of the feminine group in whose house child is reared.

Amount of diffusion through remarriage and irregular marriage of "mothers" throughout the community.

Personality of living maternal grandmothers.

Age at death of mother.

Relationship of foster mothers to own mother and to each other.

Correlate with: Personality such as aggressiveness, leadership, shyness, timidity, savoir faire, gregariousness, tendency to form wide alliances, rootlessness.

Compare these traits also with personality of fathers, foster fathers and elder brothers, probably also with "big man" of house boy.

Compare personalities of pishaben [affinal] groups; within the group.

Compare strength of marriages which do and do not follow decreed lines, in relation also to makeup of household which bride enters.

Compare brothers through different fathers, with brothers through different mothers, when mothers are clan sisters, when they aren't.

Consider primogeniture factor for both men and women. (Mead, 1933).

Here Mead is postulating a complex cluster of influences which would have important and varied emotional effects on particular Chambri men and women. In her view, Chambri men and women are like men and women in our society except that they reverse "the expectations about male-female differences so characteristic of Euro-American cultures" (Mead, 1972: 216). Her objective was to understand the characteristics of adult Chambri – the "brisk and cooperative" behavior of Chambri women, the "cattiness, jealousy, and moodiness" of Chambri men (Mead, 1972: 216) – and this objective was to be realized through reference to the process by which their subjectivities had been shaped.

This extrapolation of a Western view of persons into non-Western cultural contexts still characterizes the work of other contemporary scholars who are interested in the causes of sex-linked personality development (see Slater, 1968; Dinnerstein, 1976; Chodorow, 1971, 1974, 1979). General in scope and purporting to explain gender differences among all people, including the Chambri, these studies fail in their efforts at universality for the same reason that Mead herself failed, by remaining attached to Western cultural concepts which often distort the nature of local experience.

The following passage from Nancy Chodorow's influential

psychoanalytic study of "Family Structure and Feminine Personality" is an example of this recent work:

a crucial differentiating experience in male and female development arises out of the fact that women, universally, are largely responsible for early child care and for (at least) later female socialization. This points to the central importance of the mother-daughter relationship for women, and to a focus on the conscious and unconscious effects of early involvement with a female for children of both sexes. The fact that males and females experience this social environment differently as they grow up accounts for the development of basic sex differences in personality. (1974: 43–44)

Chodorow, therefore, would agree with Mead's suggestion that the key to personality development in both males and females is to be found "in the organization of the women's groups and the relationship of children of both sexes to women." In this respect, Mead and Chodorow each draws a portion of her theory from Freud, who, in explaining ego differentiation among both males and females, emphasizes the importance of the degree to which a child regarded its mother as nurturant (Freud: 1925).

Of greater significance, however, is the degree to which Mead and Chodorow diverge from Freud. He argues that the development of female gender identity depends on penis envy. Girls, he suggests, because they blame their mothers for their lack of penes, reject the affective bonds they have established with them and embrace, first, their fathers and, then, males in general as their source of sexual gratification. What Freud misses, however, according to both Mead and Chodorow, is the degree to which females fail to break their affective bonds with their mothers, remaining forever drawn to the "warmth of emotional tone between women."

Mead, at least with respect to the Chambri case, attributes this persistent identification of females with the "women's groups" to those social institutions which allow unity between female agnates and their female affines. Of particular importance is her reference to the "house boy [men's house] organization [which] prevents any father-daughter relationship and so decrees that a girl suffers no social weaning trauma, either in childhood or at marriage." Indeed she attributes the possession of the "real position of power in society" (1935: 256) to the strong and autonomous personalities which she sees Chambri women acquiring through their intergenerational solidarity.

Chodorow, while agreeing that women "are likely to participate in an intergenerational world with their mother, and often with their aunts and grandmother" (1974: 57), does not think that their "embeddedness" within women's groups allows them easily to assume positions of power. In fact, she argues that girls, who need not reject an early identification with their mothers in order to become adult women, may be kept "from differentiation and lessening of [their] infantile dependency" (1974: 64).

Thus, where Mead finds the aggressiveness, *savoir faire*, gregariousness and leadership ability of Chambri women, Chodorow discovers a potential for female dependence and for difficulties in individuation. However, despite the disparity of these conclusions, Mead and Chodorow remain allied in their fundamental perspective. In accounting for female personality traits both continue to rely on the same set of Western assumptions regarding individuals as subjectivities created by emotionally formative influences over time.

But Mead and Chodorow are, we think, wrong – the former explicitly and the latter by implication – in seeking to explain the relationship between Chambri men and women in terms of their personalities. If it were true that Chambri women dominate over their men, the reason would not be that mother's brother's daughter's marriage and the house boy organization allow them to become aggressive and gregarious personalities. If it were true that Chambri women lack political clout, the reason would, equally, not be that these same institutions prevent them from differentiating and from developing a mature subjectivity.

To understand whether the relationship between Chambri men and women is one of dominance, we must, it seems to us, take more accurate account of the way in which Chambri men and women actually do understand themselves. Who the Chambri consider themselves to be affects what they wish to do; and the formulation by men and women of their respective interests and strategies has a significant effect in determining the nature and patterns of their interaction. As part of our effort to describe and explain the relationship between Chambri men and women our first purpose is to understand the form dominance will assume in this society where men and women define themselves in terms of their social transactions.

Chapter 3
The enactment of power

In her analysis of male–female relations among the Chambri, Mead subscribes to the definition of dominance widely held within our culture. In this view, dominance is a relationship between individuals (or groups) in which one unjustifiably deprives the other of his or her capacity to make and enact what are regarded as reasonable decisions. Not all forms of constraint are, thus, considered expressions of dominance. Few would, for instance, interpret as dominance the insistence by a parent that his or her teenaged child eat with knife and fork.[1] To the extent that the constraints are regarded as reasonable and normal, they will be interpreted as acts of legitimate control rather than of dominance.

We recognize, of course, that there may be different perspectives within a culture on what is regarded as appropriate constraint and choice and thus different interpretations as to whether dominance has occurred. Consider the American secretary who, in the late 1950s, dressed in slacks when her boss insisted that she follow the then contemporary fashion-imperative by wearing a skirt and blouse. If she complied but only under protest, or, indeed, refused to comply at all and was subsequently fired or otherwise penalized, relatively few sympathized with her. Those who regarded the behavior of her boss as reasonable would not regard him as seeking to dominate over her; nor, therefore, would her response be interpreted as an effort to escape domination, but would be seen as irrational, perhaps the manifestation of a loss of emotional control, thought to be characteristic of women.

Others, however, would interpret the conflict between the boss and his secretary in a very different way by arguing that the culturally current definitions of what is "reasonable" and "normal" are imposed by those in power for their own benefit. These

definitions, themselves, become part of the means by which dominance is expressed and, therefore, should not be regarded as the
properly objective standards by which reasonability and normality
should be judged. That according to cultural criteria it is reasonable
and normal that most bosses are men and most secretaries are
women would, from this perspective, render invalid prevailing
cultural definitions of what constitutes reasonable and normal
standards of conduct for bosses and secretaries. Virtually any
culturally approved interaction under these circumstances between
superordinates and subordinates would be regarded as an act of
domination.

However, as divergent as these perspectives are likely to be, they,
nonetheless, reflect certain key cultural assumptions about the
nature of persons and the achievement of personal worth: from either
position it would be reasonable and normal for anyone, bosses and
secretaries included, to seek satisfaction in what they do – to establish worth as subjectivities through self-expression.[2] Moreover, from
either perspective, control of economic resources is believed essential
to achieving worth. Those who failed to sympathize with the secretary regarded the boss as reasonable for looking out for his business
interests and the secretary as irrational not only for rejecting the
dress code, but for choosing self-expression in dress at the cost of her
job, thus sacrificing the economic viability which is the most general
prerequisite for choice. Those who did sympathize with her would
sympathize with all secretaries, regarding their capacity for self-
expression both on and off the work place as contingent on, and
inherently limited by, the economic interests of others.

Our disagreement with Mead is not that she subscribed to this
general definition of dominance as an unjustifiable constraint on a
person's capacity to make and enact what could be argued are
reasonable decisions. Rather, we contend, she did not recognize that
those assumptions which even allow members of our culture to
debate whether constraint in particular cases is unjustifiable or
decisions reasonable, are not assumptions which would make sense
to the Chambri. In our view, Mead misinterpreted the bases,
mechanisms, forms and experiences of dominance among the
Chambri because she viewed men and women there in Western
terms, as subjective individuals seeking self-expression through an
economically derived individualism. Consider the following passage
from *Sex and Temperament* where she elaborates upon what she
regards as female dominance:

Here is a conflict at the very root of [a Chambri male's] psycho-sexual adjustment: his society tells him that he rules women, his experience shows him at every turn that women expect to rule him ... But the actual dominance of women is far more real than the structural position of the men, and the majority of Tchambuli young men adjust themselves to it, become accustomed to wait upon the words and desires of women. (1935: 271)

Mead implies in this passage that, if left to their own devices, Chambri men would not act as they do. She sees their behavior as an abnormality, manifesting a psycho-sexual conflict which Chambri men would like to resolve by acting according to the structural principles of their society which tell them that they should rule women. Instead, they are compelled to wait upon the words of their wives, mothers, and sisters, because it is women "who have the real position of power in society" (Mead, 1935: 253). It is women, Mead suggests, who dominate their men by compelling them to act in ways that the men, because they fail to understand the nature of power in their society, find confusing and inappropriate. That women can so compel is, moreover, a function of their control of "the underlying economics of life" (Mead, 1935: 254). Mead writes that:

For food, the people depend upon the fishing of the women ... For traded fish they obtain sago, taro, and areca-nut. And the most important manufacture, the mosquito-bags ... are made entirely by women ... And the women control the proceeds in kinas and talibun.[3] It is true that they permit the men to do the shopping, both for food at the market and in trading the mosquito-bags ... But only with the wife's approval can he spend the talibun and kina and strings of conus shells he brings back ... Real property, which one actually owns, one receives from women. (1935: 254)

Women thus, according to Mead, dominate their men because women control the significant economic resources. Men are unable to be themselves: they are forced to act against their own inclinations which in turn produces a crisis in their subjective experience of themselves – a psycho-sexual conflict which, in some cases, becomes a neurosis (see Mead, 1935: 290–309).

Mead's culturally induced error is, in our view, double. She starts with the economic sphere as distinctive and primary, whereas it is neither for the Chambri. It is socially embedded and serves as an index of social relationships rather than as a cause of social relationships (see Sahlins, 1972 and Gregory, 1982). Economics in

Chambri social life reflects, but does not determine, social relationships, including those of dominance. (Hence, the man who can make impressive affinal payments is one who knows the totemic names which control his clansmen and, thus their resources.) Moreover, the relationships of constraint prevail between those whose principal objective is not to establish themselves as distinct subjectivities but to enmesh themselves in social networks.

To be a person among the Chambri, as we have argued, is to belong to a patriclan, whose members assume corporate interests in affinal debts and credits and assert common ownership of totemic names. These names are the basis and indicators for both men and women of the social networks which afford them and their children basic identity and protection from coercion and assault. Of most importance, totemic names allow both men and women to pursue, respectively, their culturally defined preoccupations of political competition and the bearing of children.

The totemic names available to men, however, convey different sorts of powers and resources than do those available to women. The names men hold provide the possibility of gaining power over others and are the focus and basis of political competition. Men seek to augment their own power through gaining control of the names of others, as when one clan subsumes another and so acquires its ritual estate.[4] Since, for men, the social relationships between – and within – clans are manifestations of relative power, and since social relationships constitute personal identity, men define themselves primarily in terms of relative control over names – over that which gives them power.[5]

Women also define themselves by their names. However, the power conveyed by their names cannot shape social relationships as does the power of the names men hold, but, instead, ensures reproduction.[6] Because the power of women cannot be transferred into the male sphere of politics, women do not compete with men for political eminence.

The interests of Chambri men and women are not inevitably opposed (as are the interests, some would argue, of bosses and secretaries). Chambri men and women have partially distinct spheres of activity and each allows the other to pursue partially distinct strategies.[7] Consequently, women are not caught up in the politics of names, power and sorcery to make them, as a category, the usual targets of male efforts to establish power over others.[8]

Women are not, thus, to be regarded as the followers of particular men, nor are they, as was Francis Yaboli, their usual victims.[9]

If dominance can be defined as unjustifiably constraining the behavior of another by depriving him or her of the capacity to make and enact reasonable decisions, the form dominance takes among the Chambri is through the control of the social relationships and totemic powers which determine action and are the basis of Chambri identity. Moreover, a significant part of the cultural meaning of dominance for the Chambri is that only those deprived of power consider it unjustifiable that another has incapacitated them.[10] Particular cases apart, Chambri men consider it perfectly reasonable, indeed essential, given their view of entropy, that they seek to dominate over one another.

Dominance, thus, characterizes the strategies of men as they compete with each other to become equal to those who have caused them. Women, in contrast, neither compete with men nor with each other to repay their ontological debts. Yet, both men and women in their efforts to replicate those who have caused them, focus their distinctive strategies of validation on marriage, the particular social context which produced them and their relationships of primary indebtedness. Even here, where the strategies of men and women impel them to pursue their very different objectives in the same arena, it would neither be accurate to describe Chambri men as dominating Chambri women, nor, as Mead would have it, the reverse.

We begin our explication of the nature and relationships of male and female interests and strategies with the analysis of a relatively uncomplicated case of marriage, presented by Mead herself. Mead's data here are of particular interest to us, in part because they were collected from a perspective significantly different from our own about the nature of Chambri male and female interests and strategies, and thus they enable us to test our interpretations on material not of our own gathering. Moreover, if the strategies which characterized Chambri society in the 1970s and 1980s can be shown to be those which characterized Chambri society in the 1930s, just after effective European pacification, this would suggest that the strategies are organizing principles of pervasive and central importance. From Mead's unpublished field notes:

Child marriage arrangements

Late in the afternoon of March 9 ... the daughter of Tchuiape, named Mariabiendwon, was flashed [presented with valuables] and taken to the

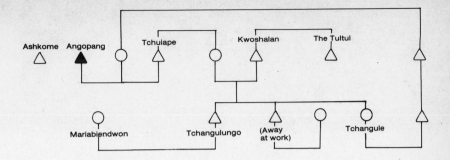

Figure 1.   Participants in child marriage arrangements

house of her betrothed, Tchangulungo, son of Kwoshalan. [See Figure 1 for the cast of primary characters.] This betrothal is of old standing, the girl is an aiyai of the boy [a woman of Tchangulungo's mother's clan] and the betrothal is dated from the time when the young husband was scarified, at which time 5 kinas were paid to his wau [mother's brother], this payment is quoted as the marking payment . . . The little girl, who is only about eleven, breasts mere nipples, and a scrawny ugly little thing, was flashed by distant "brothers," Werebango and Kaviwan. The flash was provided by the girl's "Father" [aso], individual unit contributions being also made by Monolable, Yaponakin, and Mamandi. As she had never been cut [scarified], she had no flash given her by her wau.[11] The flash which is hung up intact in a billum [net bag] which went with it and which belongs to the girl and will be given by her to her son, was meagre and consisted of: a skull cap of netting with a few gams [bailer shells] tied to it, 1 long string of native buttons, a string of 6 gams, 2 leglets of me [small cowry shells], a lime gourd slightly flashed with me, 2 short strings of European buttons, a string of 10 sliced gams, a huge cut gam, 1 string of large old buttons, 3 ovalis shells. The girl was escorted to the house by her distant brothers, Kaviwan, Werebango and some young boys. Her young husband can no longer stay in the house, which is small, but sleeps in the house of Tchangule [his sister, whose husband is Mariabiendwon's mother's brother]. She sleeps with her sister-in-law, wife of another son of Kwoshalan who is away at work. The wife of the TT [the *Tultul*, the Administration imposed position of assistant village leader, in this case Kwoshalan's brother] and his sister-in-law each gave her a fireplace [clay hearth], which is customary for the women married into the house to contribute to the new bride. Later she will weave herself a sleeping bag. When she is finally really married, her folk will give her a complete set of cooking pots. She can now weave tchi [mosquito bags], head mats and fans, and fish. The girl sat the next

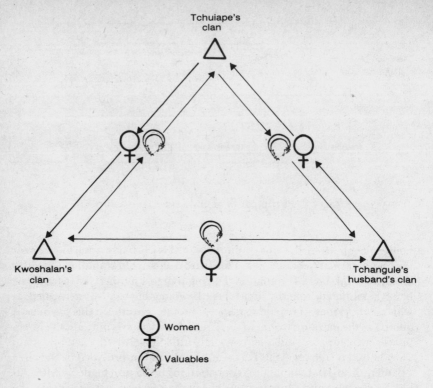

Figure 2.   Mother's brother's daughter's marriage

morning next to her fireplace, sponging her sore eyes with a piece of muli
[a citrus fruit], they were sore from the paint and oil which had gotten
into them. She was sulkily shy, refused to talk at all, and when the TT
asked her who had flashed her went and whispered the answer to her
sister-in-law.

This girl is really the daughter of Angopang of Kilimbit who was
killed by Palimbai [speakers of a Iatmul dialect]. He had promised the
girl to Ashkome [of Indingai] for Taukumbank. Then when Angopang
was killed, the girl's mother remarried to Tchuiape of Olimbit [a
Kilimbit men's house], who flouted the previous betrothal and betrothed her to Kwoshalan's son. The morning the payment was sent,
Mar, 10, Ashkome arrived at Olimbit HB [house boy] and claimed
damages. Tchuiape explained that his action was so the girl wouldn't
marry into a faraway place, and gave Ashkome a handsome string of
gams – these were not from the bride price which was 2 kinas, 1 breast
plate shell, 1 string me and 3 terubumb [green snail shells]. (Mead,
1933)

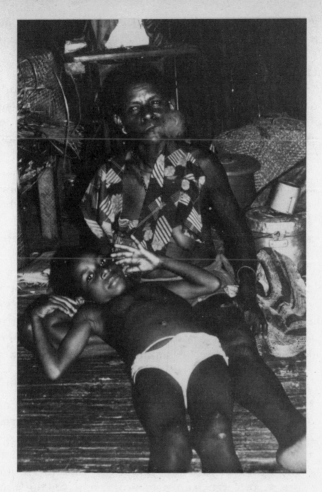

Photograph 2. Women can, in fact, directly replicate them-selves

Mariabiendwon's betrothal to Tchangulungo was, by Chambri standards, a simple case of mother's brother's daughter's marriage, involving the three clans of Tchuiape, Kwoshalan, and Tchangule's husband. Women moved in one direction: from Tchuiape's to Kwoshalan's clan, from Kwoshalon's clan to Tchangule's hus-band's and from Tchangule's husband's clan to Tchuiape's clan. Valuables moved in the opposite direction, in exchange for these women and their future children. (See Figure 2). Thus Mead describes Kwolshalan and his younger brother, the *Tultul*, giving a marking payment and a bride-price to Tchuiape, as undoubtedly they had received similar payments from the members of Tchangule's husband's clan, upon Tchangule's betrothal and marriage.

Rather than supporting Mead's conclusion that Chambri women dominated their men, her description of the marriage of this rather pathetic little girl suggests the opposite. However, this conclusion would also be misleading because in expressing their ambitions, the men were not necessarily dominating the women. Even though the bride appeared other than radiant and even though Mead makes no mention of any woman having a say in these arrangements, the conclusion does not follow that women were under the domination of their men. Indeed, it is just this form of mother's brother's daughter's marriage that both men and women may find satisfactory because it allows members of both groups to validate themselves.

Women can, in fact, most directly replicate themselves if their descendants return to the social positions from which the women themselves originated. When a pattern of mother's brother's daughter's marriage is followed, a woman's descendants are married into the various groups which produced her parents. For instance, Mariabiendwon's daughter's daughter would eventually assume the social position of Mariabiendwon's own mother and Mariabiendwon would, thus, in this closed system, have caused her own existence. Her male descendants, in a roughly comparable manner, would come to replace those who gave her mother in marriage.

It is, however, unlikely that Mariabiendwon realized that mother's brother's daughter's marriage furthered her interests in precisely this way, although she and other Chambri women do, indeed, express a preference for sisters marrying into the same clan. Because sisters share the same set of social relationships under these circumstances, their identification with each other is likely to be particularly close. Living with their sisters and surrounded by children who call each woman "mother," these women can experience themselves on a daily basis as creating and perpetuating an intergenerational kin group. Although women can reproduce themselves in the most general way simply by having (or adopting) children of either sex, the strongest and most enduring sense of self-replication comes from a marriage arrangement which results in the circulation of a woman's descendants within a closed marriage system.[12]

Men, like women, wish to repay their ontological debts and, in so doing, compete with each other in an effort to replicate the power of those who have produced them. When they fear that they are losing power as a result of this competition, they sometimes choose the arrangements of mother's brother's daughter's marriage that is always so satisfactory to women.

Nearly 30 per cent of Chambri patriclans did contract all of their marriages with their mother's brother's clans, according to both Mead's data collected in 1933 and Deborah's data collected in 1974. Clans which followed this form of marriage were similar to those concerned with the marriage of Mariabiendwon. From Mead's description, none had sufficient power to muster impressive marriage payments. Indeed, their viability depended on their coordinating carefully the occasions on which they had to make affinal payments with those on which they would receive them. Marriages, birth payments, initiations, and funerals had to be timed so that income could be precisely balanced with expenditure. Since women and valuables move in opposite directions within the closed system of mother's brother's daughter's marriage, the rate of flow of each is interdependent and subject to some regulation by each of the three participating clans. However, clans which hope to maintain their autonomy through mother's brother's daughter's marriage are rarely powerful enough to weather disruptions in coordination brought on, most frequently, by demographic imbalances: most, eventually, become the clients of more powerful clans (see Gewertz, 1982).

Fortune, in his description of mother's brother's daughter's marriage among the Chambri, appreciated the simplicity of a marriage system in which it was "impossible for a man to marry a woman without his creating a lien in perpetuity upon the male line she comes from in favor of his male descendants" (1933b: 3). Nevertheless, such a lien, as the statistics just cited show, was far from binding. (Nor does the Chambri ideal of patrimoiety exogamy serve to greatly restrict marriage choice since this rule is followed only 60 per cent of the time.) Wife-givers often rejected the obligation of marital precedent in order more easily to marry their daughters to powerful clansmen who would pay large bride-prices and maintain a high level of affinal exchange. Important wife-takers, on their part, often asserted comparable independence so that they could display their success by marrying women from prestigious clans. To the extent that members of a powerful clan could marry as they liked – "marry around," as the Chambri phrase it – the wider would be their sphere of influence. Thus during one debate, the men asserted that "even if affines 'carry' the child [support him during various rituals], the child can still marry where he and his fathers like" [not necessarily marry a member of his mother's brother's daughter's clan]; or, "I'll fight anyone who tells me where my daughter should marry."

But what does this propensity to marry around on the part of Chambri men mean to Chambri women, who have a strong affective preference for sisters marrying into the same clan? Since men do arrange most marriages, they might appear to control women through their capacity to separate sisters. Several kinds of data suggest, however, that if this control exists, it has little serious consequence.

The nature of Chambri settlement ensures that sisters will rarely live far from each other. Chambri Island is rather small, with the houses of the approximately 1,000 residents within easy walking distance of one another. Indeed, it is a matter of no more than a 30-minute walk from the first house of the westernmost village of Wombun to the last house of the easternmost village of Kilimbit. Since most Chambri marry other Chambri (with a frequency of 91 per cent in 1974) seldom will women experience great separation from each other or from any of their kin after marriage.

Moreover, few men have the resources necessary even to marry into another Chambri village.[13] (See Table 1 for frequency of village endogamy during 1933 and 1974.) It is much more difficult for a man to become known as an important man outside his home village than it is within it. His kin group must indeed be powerful for his affinal presentations to be large enough to impress those who do not feel his influence on a daily basis. In addition, since such a marriage involves members of different villages, it becomes something of an affair of state with the reputation of the entire village riding not only on his performance but also on that of his clan.

Most Chambri women, thus, who do not actually live with their sisters in the same house or adjacent houses need walk for only a few minutes within their village to be with their clanswomen. Even those few women married outside their village to such exceptionally important men have only a short walk in order to visit their sisters and to participate with them in ceremonies. None are, in these respects, seriously thwarted in the realization of their objectives by the aspirations of men.[14]

But a woman is not to be understood as only escaping male

Table 1 *The frequency of endogamous marriage at Chambri during 1933 and 1974*

					% of Endogamy	
Village	Indingai	Kilimbit	Wombun	Non-Chambri	Village	All-Chambri
1933						
Indingai	23	4	1	2	82	93
Kilimbit	7	18	1	0	69	100
Wombun	4	0	12	0	75	100
1974						
Indingai	64	11	6	7	73	92
Kilimbit	13	94	2	11	78	92
Wombun	6	1	86	11	83	90

The 1933 figures were derived from Margaret Mead's unpublished censuses. They are incomplete, reflecting her partial conclusion of the work. The per cent of extratribal marriages was actually higher in 1933, because the Chambri had intermarried with members of Sepik Hills groups during their exile among them from about 1905 to 1927. See Gewertz, 1983, for a full discussion of this exile. The 1974 figures were collected by Deborah. They were calculated from the male perspective to avoid double-counting, and include the marriages of migrant laborers.

dominance through geographical or socioeconomic accident. She can also take an effective role in choosing her husband, and in most cases she receives agnatic support for her choice. In particular, she – and her male agnates – will try to choose a man with sufficient ancestral power so that she and her children will have the necessities of life and will remain healthy. (As we will see in Chapter 5, her sexual attraction to a potential husband is understood as a measure of his totemic power, the same power that will enable him to support her and her children.) After all she will not be able to have the satisfaction of replacing those who caused her if she and her children die prematurely. Indeed, she may require the help of her children, particularly of her sons, in her declining years.[15]

The processes through which women can prevent men from compromising women's strategies will become more apparent in later chapters: all play upon the anxiety men experience over the capacity women have to assist others in acquiring the totemic names of their husbands. Thus, no man wishes to marry a woman whose antipathy is so strong that she is likely to betray him. Women, thus, can usually ensure that their interests are met: in most cases, the marriage preferences of men enable women – even the shy little Mariabiendwon – to pursue satisfactorily their own objectives; in other instances, women can veto the choices of the men.[16]

Chambri men and women are able to recognize and appraise the social pattern that is created through the intersection of their interests and strategies, and they do analyze the nature of their social order. This is the topic of our next chapter.

Chapter 4
The construction of society

Our concern, thus far, has been to distill the principles through which Chambri men and women organize and experience their lives. In this chapter, we complete our exposition of these principles by examining the commentary the Chambri themselves make about their social order.[1] The clearest statements in Chambri political theory concerning the nature and relationship of male and female interests and the strategies they generate appear in the form of certain myths which present images of social life that contrast sharply with the normal Chambri pattern. Significantly, even when Chambri speculate through these myths about the possible ways in which their society might be changed, they still assume that the interests of men and women will necessarily remain distinct. Indeed, in the first and second of the following three myths, the interests of men and women are pursued in strategies so divergent that men and women are separated into distinct societies. That these societies prove ultimately to be inadequate suggests that they are only partial and that, therefore, men and women must learn to accommodate themselves to each other within a more complete – within a single – society. However, as the third myth shows, even when men and women do accommodate themselves to each other within a single society, this accommodation may be disastrously imperfect.

The myth of the Golden Girl: the partial society of undifferentiated men

We Chambri were the first to learn the secret of flying, but then we forgot what we had learned. Palimal was the man who learned how, after he had killed the [kind of] big black bird we call Nomande. He stripped the bird of its feathers and placed them in the sun to dry. When they were thoroughly dried, he put them on his body as one does a shirt. With them on he could jump up to the branch of a tree. His second jump brought him to the top of the tree. And by the third try, he could soar through the sky.

Now Palimal had a younger brother named Malu. Both men belonged to the Wiarmanagwi men's house at Indingai. One day all of the men assembled there to see a woman emerge from the ground. She had skin the color of gold, and all of the men had intercourse with her after they brought her some food.

Her name was Kupkinchishilkinemenan [literally, the underground woman] and when the men left her in the morning to find food, they placed her in a *karuka* [a trough used in gold mining] and covered her with a tarpaulin.

Soon their wives became suspicious because they had not been visited by their husbands for a long time. One day the wives of Palimal and Malu were drawing water near Wiarmanagwi. As they filled their water gourds they saw the golden woman's reflection in the pool. The men had forgotten to cover her with the tarpaulin.

The two women called together all of the women who had married into Wiarmanagwi. The leader of these women was Yepikanimbur. After she learned that no husband had been interested in intercourse recently, she ordered the women to fetch axes and spears and to follow her. When they came to the men's house, they stabbed the Golden Girl, leaving her bloody remains in the *karuka*.

Elsewhere Deborah has discussed the Golden Girl story as relating to a particular era in Chambri history (Gewertz, 1985). The myth, after all, does refer to the time after Chambri began to work on plantations and at gold mines. The goldenness of the girl is appreciated as valuable; the men hide her in a trough used by miners; they cover her with a tarpaulin. Yet, these historically contingent experiences are given cultural meaning within a story which is fundamentally about male-female relationships.[2]

That Kupkinchishilkinemenan is golden means that she is not only a woman but a valuable. She, thus, embodies at the same time both sides of affinal exchange. In so doing, we will argue, she confounds the distinction between wife-givers and wife-takers, which provides the basis of the competition between men.

Central to the politics of affinal exchange is the Chambri perception that women are similar yet distinct from the items given in exchange for them. A modern affinal presentation takes the form of a "money tree" which consists of many low-denomination bank notes, often numbering in the hundreds, attached to sticks which are then thrust into the spine of a sago palm frond. This variety of palm frequently represents women in Chambri mythology, in contrast to the essentially male coconut palm. Each money tree, moreover, is decorated with a *bilum*, the kind of net bag used by Chambri women to carry their infants. Money trees are frequently displayed in a line, particularly during male initiation ceremonies when many mother's brothers are receiving affinal reimbursements. As one looks at these, one sees represented a row of women, about to be given to the wife-givers.

The shell valuables of *kina*, *lin* and *talimbun*, used by the Chambri before they transacted in currency to acquire wives and recompense matrilateral kinsmen, also represent women. The *talimbun* shell, for instance, is explicitly associated with wombs.[3] During male initiation ceremonies, for instance, when mothers, mothers' sisters, and sisters of the young initiates use these shells to rinse the body paint from the initiates, they refer to the water they contain as the blood within their wombs.

That valuables which represent not only women, but often their wombs, are exchanged in affinal presentations for wives suggests both that wives are in this context defined as important because of their wombs and that Chambri men wish to achieve close equivalence with each other. Yet, since representations of human wombs do not, after all, reproduce humans, valuables remain an inadequate, although appropriate, payment for wives. Because of the ineluctable difference between women and valuables, wife-takers remain, despite the generosity of their affinal payments, less than the equal of their wife-givers. The significance of the Golden Girl, thus, as the merging of valuable and woman, is that she appeals to the interests of Chambri men by enticing them with the prospect of freedom from affinal and, moreover, from agnatic inequality.

That the Golden Girl is both valuable and woman is consistent with her origin from the ground as her own first cause. She is no one's daughter or sister and, since she belongs to no clan, cannot be claimed by, or given to, any clan. She, therefore, establishes no distinctions between affines. In addition, she is no one's wife or mother and as a consequence agnatic and generational differences dissolve. Because Kupkinchishilkinemenan did not have to – indeed, could not – be exchanged, she established no distinctions between the men of Wiarmanagwi men's house who had intercourse with her and who hid her from their wives. She allows all of the men of the Wiarmanagwi men's house to remain together – men who, if they were like those of the Wiarmanagwi we knew, belonged to five different clans, each of which had representatives from one and sometimes both of the inter-marrying moieties, as well as from several generations. She achieves this unification of the men by terminating the relationships they had with their wives and, thus, with their affines and agnates. She is all the men need, and they would have been happy to remain together – undifferentiated as affines, agnates and members of different generations – if only their wives would have allowed it.[4]

The partial society of men living in unity apart from their wives which is established by the advent of the Golden Girl exists, as we have seen, within the men's house. The men's house is more than a convenient retreat for men, more than a place where men may escape from their wives: it is the embodiment of central male socio-cosmic relationships. There, men enact the critical social distinctions of their lives as they participate together in debates, marriage arrangements, shamanistic seances, ceremonies and, in the past, war councils. It is a building which itself conveys these same social distinctions. The posts which support the house are carved by men of particular clans who, when incising their own totemic markings upon them, recite the sacred names which imbue the house supports with their patrilineal powers. These posts and other architectural features provide the physical markers which determine where the men will sit as they give themselves social definition through their clans and ceremonial moieties.

The men's house, however, as a structure imbued with totemic significance and spatial distinction, is not merely a setting that mirrors those activities which take place within it: it is a setting that affects those activities. Bateson's (1946) description of the "assertive art" of the Middle Sepik helps us understand this view of efficacy. This art has as its basic theme:

a sort of immanent totemism. The crocodiles, weevils, and ancestors with noble noses are the people who made them and the people who admired them ... In every village you will find the living embodiments of the ancient mythology – the man who bears the name of the founder of the village. He will straighten his shoulders as he tells you "I steered the canoe which brought my clan to this place." And another man will stamp on the ground as he says "I am Kevembuangga. I put my foot on the mud and made it hard so that people could live. But for me there would be no people. There would be no pigs.

... Every one of the [art] items ... had its ancestral personal names referring back to mythology but also borne by someone living in the village.

One other aspect of this art must be mentioned. The objects are ... associated with the great men's ceremonial houses which are characteristic of the area. ... The interior of the ceremonial house is ... referred to as its "belly" and the ceremonial house is itself female. Each such house is a female ancestor whose gigantic face appears on the gable font and whose name is given to the building as a whole. The masculine assertive art thus has its locus within a grandiose female matrix. (Bateson, 1946: 121)

There is no difference, as Bateson makes clear, between the ancestral Kevembuangga, the art objects that personify him, the names which invoke him, and the man who holds these objects and owns and employs these names. In this world of totemic identities, moreover, Kevembuangga becomes who he is through the activities of establishing his social position, acquiring and employing ancestral objects and names.[5] Because he is Kevembuangga he dons the mask of the ancestral Kevembuangga; because he is able to don this mask, he becomes this ancestor.

Comparably, the men become those distinctions marked by the structure of their ceremonial house and embody those distinctions through their displays, debates and seances. They also acquire an identity because they meet within a house which at the same time is a "grandiose female matrix." Supported by posts demarcating the clans and patrimoieties which join together within her "belly," she nonetheless encompasses and so transcends these social categories.[6] Although only one of many ceremonial houses within a village, each called by exoteric names like Wiarmanagwi, Mindimbit, or Abraragwi and by esoteric names known only to those who meet within her, she is unrelated to any other. Nor is she subsumed or dispersed as no one bears her names but herself, and no other objects contain her powers.

As the undifferentiated mother of the men who reside within her, she is the belly which by enveloping distinction precludes both entropy and ontological debt. The differences which divide agnates into seniors and juniors and divide wife-givers from wife-takers remain nascent: while her sons remain within her – while they meet in her body to display, debate, negotiate – they remain in the world of potentiality, of assertion alone. Only in the world outside the men's house do the exchanges take place through which differences are actually established, obligations actually acknowledged and power actually displayed, transferred and lost.

It is within this world of men who are equal only while their differences and obligations remain nascent that the members of Wiarmanagwi seclude their Golden Girl. As *sui generis* and valuable merged with woman, she has not been and cannot be acquired through exchange; she neither divides nor obligates the men. And because she is a woman, rather than merely a representation of a woman, she conveys the possibility of self-sufficiency. With the Golden Girl, the men hope to remain within the womb of their men's house, reproducing themselves but not their social differences and obligations.[7]

The women, however, wonder why their husbands are ignoring them for such a long time. When they discover the Golden Girl, they recognize that they have indeed become entirely superfluous to the men: the men have decided to pursue their own selfish interests and disregard the interests of women, which are expressed in bearing children. Together the wives of the Wiarmanagwi men, led by Yepikanimbur, slay Kupkinchishilkinemenan and thus shatter the partial society of the men's house. Their action is impelled by the logic of Chambri sexual strategy: while the Golden Girl remains in the men's house, women will not be able to repay their ontological debts. Chambri women can become self-contained as long as their husbands are not.

A myth of Tsimtsan: the partial society of undifferentiated women

Only while women are at Chambri, however, do they continue to need their husbands. As the events which follow immediately upon the death of the Golden Girl indicate, a partial society composed only of women is also a possible construction of the Chambri social imagination:

Yepikanimbur then prepared a soup in the bowl called Kamburulan. After all of the women drank it, they turned into the birds we call *kambu* and flew to the bush near Kamchua.[8]

When the men came back and found the Golden Girl dead, they also made a soup, turned into bats and flew to Suapmeri on the river.[9] Palimal told Malu not to eat the soup, that Palimal could teach his younger brother to fly without the soup's power. After making another set of wings for his brother, Palimal and Malu flew off to find their wives.

As they approached Kamchua, Palimal warned Malu not to have intercourse with his wife. If he did so, then the magic would not work and he would be unable to fly back to Chambri. But Malu did not listen to Palimal. He slept with his wife and when Yepikanimbur came to check the beds of all the women, she, their leader, found and killed him. But Palimal and his wife escaped back to Chambri. He held her under his wing as he flew across the lake.

The perspective of the women with regard to their husbands has significantly changed. While living on Chambri Island, the wives killed the Golden Girl because their husbands *did not* have sex with them; subsequently, on Kamchua, a husband is killed because he *did* have sex with his wife. By killing Malu, women repudiate the male initiative to resume the relations characteristic of normal society. With the exception of Palimal's wife who returned with him to Chambri, these women thus demonstrate that they no longer wish men to provide them with anything. They then show, moreover, that they can supersede the old society by constructing a new one in which they are able to pursue their interests with complete disregard of the men. In the sequel to the story of Golden Girl, the women move from Kamchua to form a community of Tsimtsan, deep in the Sepik Hills. There they continue to live happily and successfully without any men at all.[10]

Because no men live at Tsimtsan, we were told, there is no sexual division of labor. Each woman living there does everything for herself.[11] Indeed, she reproduces by herself. When she wishes to conceive, she lies on her back, high on a mountain top, and opens her vulva to the wind. If she bears a male child, she destroys it. If she bears a female child, she lets it live. And so, the society of women reproduces itself, with each woman pledged to kill any man she comes upon.

That these women at Tsimtsan are successful in reproducing themselves without men marks them both as self-sufficient and as undifferentiated by patrilineage. Because conception is through the agency of the wind (which Chambri men, at least, regard as entirely possible), children born at Tsimtsan do not have the patrilineal imprint conveyed through semen and the movements of repeated acts of sexual intercourse.[12] As a consequence, mothers and daughters – as well, of course, as wives and sisters – are not separated from each other through the distinction of clan membership. Since the only essential difference between women would be in generation, women would redeem themselves from ontological debt through the simple process of generational succession. Hence, in this depiction of Tsimtsan, women are readily and reliably able to pursue their interests of achieving the reproductive continuity denied them while the men remained with the Golden Girl.[13]

Perhaps appropriately, one of our accounts of Tsimtsan was presented by several men who were constructing a rather abbreviated men's house. One of these concluded this story – and, indeed, summarized both stories – by telling us that these women at Tsimtsan do not like men because "when they lived at Chambri, their husbands did not act as men are supposed to act towards their wives. They did not provide them with canoes, nor build them houses, nor visit them at night, and so the women thought, 'what good are men anyway?' "

The implication of these two myths, thus, is that the interests of *both* men and women can be adequately served only if there is sufficient compromise so that the strategies of one sex do not completely exclude those of the other. Nonetheless, the actual degree of accommodation required may remain subject to dispute as this third myth about the division of labor indicates.

The myth of Tangwilyeris and Tangwimangowi: on men's houses and the division of labor

Mianbanmeli was hungry. His mother, Tangwilyeris, busy weaving a mosquito bag, had not given him any fish, so he said to her: "Mama, if you go and get me some fish, I'll tell you all of father's secret names."

She went to get the fish, not knowing that Tangwimangowi, while resting inside his mosquito bag, had heard the offer his son had made to his wife.

That night when Tangwimangowi went into the men's house, he beat the *garamut* [slit gong drum] to summon the members of his clan. He beat the *garamut* and it cried: "Come to the Tangwiman men's house. Come quickly. There is trouble." Many members of his clan were already there, having worked to repair the men's house during the day. They were tired, but became enraged when they heard what Tangwimangowi had to say.

This is what he said: "You men, listen to me. My son, Mianbanmeli, has revealed that which we have kept covered up. He did this to flatter his mother, to please her so that she would bring him fish."

After they heard Tangwimangowi's speech, they began to sharpen their spears. All night they worked on them, and by the morning, the spears were ready.

They called to Mianbanmeli. They asked him to help them uncover the image of their patrimoiety which they had hung, shrouded by leaves, under the eaves of the men's house at one of its gable ends. It was his own father who asked him to help them. But his father was really helping the other men to trick his son.

The men had placed their sharpened spears around the men's house, and had removed most of the beams which supported the eaves. When Mianbanmeli climbed up to uncover the image, part of the structure collapsed, and he fell on the spears, crying? "Oh, papa, you're not like a father should be. I don't think I'm really your son." After he said this, Mainbanmeli died.

Tangwilyeris ran, screaming into the village: "He did not tell me anything. I know nothing more than this about your clan," at which point she began to sing some of the secret names of her husband's ancestral spirits.

Tangwilyeris went home to her brothers. She left her husband and stayed with her brothers until she died. Tangwimangowi did not have the power to get her back. Soon he died too. He died all by himself. He died alone, without a wife and without a son.

The myth of Tangwilyeris and Tanwimangowi was told to us by Sapui, our best female informant, in response to our question of why women are excluded from the Chambri men's houses. The story she gave as her answer depicts a conventional Chambri sexual division of labor, with Tangwilyeris weaving a mosquito bag, while Tanwimangowi and his agnates repair their men's house. However, as each calamity suggests, the division of labor requires not only that the activities of men and women be distinct but that they be employed to sustain the right sorts of social relationships. The work of women must be separate from that of men and should include not only catching fish, but feeding children; the work of men must be separate as well and should include not only repairing ceremonial houses but transmitting ritual knowledge to sons.

Both Tangwilyeris and Tangwimangowi are perversions of Chambri women and men.[14] Tangwilyeris went to get food for her son in order to gain access to more of her husband's totemic secrets.[15] In doing so, she lost the opportunity her son provided her to become a Chambri woman of.worth, and returned to her brothers to die alone. In his turn, Tangwimangowi offered his son ritual development only in order to kill him: Luring him to the men's house through the promise of agnatic privilege as the man chosen to reveal the newly completed image of the patrimoiety, Tangwimangowi elevated his son only to cause his downfall. If he had incorporated Mianbanmeli into the ritual of life of their patriclan – if Mianbanmeli had located his identity within the patriclan – then the tragedy would not have occurred. Mianbanmeli would never have flattered his mother with the promise of totemic secrets if he had thought these secrets significant. By refusing to grant his son an understanding of their importance, Tangwimangowi, too, lost the chance of becoming a Chambri of worth. With the death of his son, he lost an agnate who could give him effective support in his affinal exchanges. Moreover, his wife further dissipated his powers by revealing many of his secret names. He died without even the efficacy to recall her from her brothers, and certainly without the additional powers he would have needed to repay those to whom he was indebted.

These themes replicate, on a smaller scale, those of the first two myths: both Tangwilyeris and Tangwimangowi attempt to shape all activity to conform with their interests. As in the myth of Tsimtsan, her interests encompass all existing social domains; as in the myth of the Golden Girl, his interests cause him to resist obligation.

The myths of the Golden Girl and Tsimtsan and the behavior of Tangwimangowi and Tangwilyeris, although symmetrical, are not equally probable as extensions of male and female interests. Although their seclusion with the Golden Girl and Tangwimango-wi's denial of differentiation through withholding ritual knowledge from his son have considerable appeal to men as strategies, their seclusion at Tsimtsan and Tangwilyeris' coercion of her son to gain ritual knowledge have less appeal to women as strategies.

Only with reluctance do men act together in clans to educate their agnates in ritual knowledge and to compensate their affines: they long to be able to achieve equality through gaining release from their social obligations. Indeed, if the men had a Tsimtsan available to them they would move there. Chambri women, however, are considerably more willing to pursue a strategy of achieving worth which accepts marriage and affinal obligations. Moving to Tsim-tsan appeals to them primarily as a retaliation for the encroachment of male strategies on their own. Consequently, while some Chambri men may think Tangwimangowi wise for having denied his ritual secrets to a son as indiscreet as Mianbanmeli, no woman – this side of Tsimtsan – would be likely to judge Tangwilyeris as anything but foolish for so quickly judging that the welfare of her son was irrelevant to her own.

On a consensual society

The death of the Golden Girl impels Chambri men to accept their existing social world. The perpetual seclusion of men in the men's house never held much hope of practicality as a strategy because in the normal course of events, valuables are not wombs and every woman is someone's daughter. And, although as a feasible trans-formation of normal Chambri society Tsimtsan is still thought to exist, few Chambri women would choose to abandon their kin to set out on such a difficult trip.[16] That men and women each are willing to relinquish the active pursuit of the strategies manifested in alternative societies forms the basis of a social contract which reads metaphorically: we women will not move to Tsimtsan if you men will come out of your ceremonial houses. However, as the third myth suggests, the pressures which necessitated this social contract may lead, if not to its revocation, then to its evasion.

These three myths together specify not only the nature of key elements of Chambri society but also those arrangements of these elements which, however appealing to some, are fundamentally flawed. The myths delineate the boundaries of the socially possible within which Chambri men and women must learn to live. The difficult process through which Chambri men and women accommodate their interests and strategies – Chambri sexual politics – is the focus of our remaining chapters.

Part two

Social action

Chapter 5
Politics and the relationship between husbands and wives

In the story of the Golden Girl, of the women at Tsimtsan, and of Tangwilyeris and Tangwimangowi, the Chambri explore possible relationships between male and female strategies. By presenting themselves with images in which one strategy is pursued to the extent that it excludes the other, they can appraise the alternatives inherent in the logic of their culture.[1] However, they find the Golden Girl to be dead, the route to Tsimtsan, obscure, and so recognize from these mythic discourses in political theory that men and women must negotiate their interests within the everyday world of affinal politics and children.

We have chosen to begin our discussion of this process of negotiation with an account from Mead's field notes of a perplexing dispute over a disgruntled wife. This case conveys the complexity of Chambri political intrigue, which often pervades and shapes the relationship between husbands and wives.

Details of the deja vue repeat quarrel. Mar. 7

The wife of Mandjinakwon [Wenente], who lives with Ashkome, in Mandjinakwon's absence at work, had a quarrel with the wife of Ashkome, which began in the wife of Mandjinakwon shoving away the child of the wife of Ashkome. [See Figure 3 to clarify the relationships between those mentioned in this case.] Wife of Ashkome replied, "why do you act like that? We two live in one house. Children are not plentiful. Should you not give food to this my child and treat it well?" From these mild reproaches she turned to bitterer ones and demanded back her terubumb [*talimbun*].

The wife of Mandjinakwon either believed or pretended to believe that this was a demand back for the bride-price which had been paid for her. She went to Kilimbit, to the house of Kashibonga's wau [mother's brother], who is married to the woman who was the wife of Mandjinakwon's [Wenente's] co-wife when she [Wenente] was married to another of

71

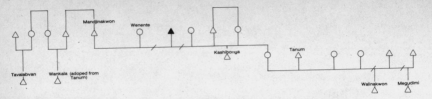

Figure 3.   Participants in the deja vue repeat quarrel

Kashibonga's waus, now dead. She told her troubles to her former co-wife, complaining that Ashkome was always abusing her and demanding back his pay.

Kashibonga was in the HB [ceremonial house] and was summoned up: He heard what she had to say, but says he replied: "Why do you come to us? We did not receive any of the pay when you were remarried. All the pay which my wau spent for you was lost nothing, and your father and brothers took all of it.[2] Why don't you go and tell them your troubles?"

The wife of Mandjinakwon returned home. The next day Kashibonga ... set out to investigate the matter.[3] He came to Yangaraman [a men's house] and enquired for Ashkome and was told he was in his house, and Tanum said: "Why not go up and see him there?"

Kashibonga went up and remained a long time; he ate taro, he drank water, it was a long time before he explained the reason for his coming. He enquired for the wife of Mandjinakwon, and Ashkome said she was in another house weaving a basket. Finally Kashibonga cautiously explained his coming. (Tavalabvan was sent for at this point. Why still not clear.)

Ashkome denied any intention of returning the woman and the cause of the quarrel was explained, and that the wife of Ashkome had referred not to the bride-price but to four terubumb which she had contributed to pay for a cutting [scarification] of the child of the wife of Mandjinakwon, said child now dead.

Kashibonga went home satisfied, but the next day Taukumbank came back from Nyaula [a Iatmul dialect group], heard that Kashibonga had been up to the house enquiring about the matter and flew into a boiling rage, summoned a court at the house kiap [the house occupied by the patrol officer when he visits the village]. The Tultul, Kashibonga, Tavalabvan the DB [medical orderly], the wife of Ashkome, and the wife of Mandjinakwon came. Wife of Ashkome explained the story all over again, the wife of Mandjinakwon scolded, Kashibonga explained why he had come, and what he had said, and Ashkome sat on the side lines and said it was alright, it was alright, he didn't want the pay back, who was enough to pay back all he had paid for her, he wished to keep her. But Taukumbank still raged and said he would put a court against Kashibonga for coming up to the house instead of seeing Ashkome in the house boy.

I [Mead] tried to get to the root of the trouble. "Hadn't Ashkome been in the house when Kashibonga came?" Yes. "Well what was the quarrel then, it wasn't as if there had only been women in the house?" He had no right to come into the house. "But Ashkome was there." Ashkome sat down like a child and did not resent it. But he Taukumbank had come to resent it, and he'd make a court. Then the DB muttered as an aside that Tanum had told Kashibonga to go up, that Ashkome was in his house. So I tried this on an unappeased Taukumbank. "Who is the big man, you or Tanum?" Tanum. "Alright, did you know that when Kashibonga came to look for Ashkome, Tanum told him to go up to the house?" Oh – he collapsed, uttered, muttering. Then he came over and told me why he had been so angry.

It seems that they had paid for a wife for Mandjinakwon before, and that in the course of what looked like innocent negotiations a titular "brother" [of the bride], Megudimi, had "gone up to the house married [where the couple were living] instead of talking in the "house boy" and subsequently, the woman had run away and married Walinakwon. Therefore, because Kashibonga, acting for the girl's kin, had gone up to the house married, this wife of Mandjinakwon would be lost also. (1933)

Mead seems to have misunderstood the cause of Taukumbank's rage. Certainly her efforts to placate what she took to be his fears about the sexual accessibility of the wife of Mandjinakwon were unsuccessful: he failed to derive reassurance from Mead's statement that Ashkome's presence in the house would almost certainly have precluded adultery. Since adultery should no longer have been an issue, Mead found Taukumbank's reactions inappropriate and regarded his "boiling rage" as unjustified. Indeed, later she diagnosed him as "maladjusted" (1935: 272).

Taukumbank does, in fact, indicate rather directly what is making him angry: he knew that adultery could not have taken place but was nonetheless concerned because, he explicitly tells Mead, Mandjinakwon had once before lost his wife to another man. Moreover, that he takes no comfort from Mead's reminder that Tanum, the big man of Yangaraman men's house, had involved himself in the case suggests that Tanum's interest in the woman may well have been related to the cause of Taukumbank's anger. Perhaps the reason he "collapsed, uttered, muttering" was not because Mead's logic was unassailable, but because he knew, or wished to indicate, that he was under an attack in which Tanum and the loss of Mandjinakwon's previous wife played a role.

What Mead did not understand was that the political viability of the group to which Mandjinakwon belonged was at stake and not just the sexual fidelity of his wife. Mead's focus on adultery was in this case, as we shall see, too narrow.[4] We need to look more closely into the relationships among Ashkome, Mandjinakwon, Taukumbank and Tanum to understand why an attack was assumed and into the Chambri view of the relationship between husband and wife to understand why an attack took this form.

Mead refers to Ashkome, Mandjinakwon and Taukumbank in her field notes as "runaways" – individuals who moved from one men's house to another because they were changing their patriclan affiliation.[5] According to her household surveys and our genealogies, Ashkome and Mandjinakwon were full brothers and had been members of the Ashanapwan patriclan.[6] Taukumbank had belonged to the Yapanunk clan but all three, as members of two residentially proximate clans, had been affiliated with the Mongeimbit men's house. Shortly before Mead's arrival, all three changed their clan membership and became members of the Mongemali clan of Tanum which met in the Yangaraman men's house.

We can reconstruct only the most general reasons why Ashkome, Mandjinakwon and Taukumbank moved. Tanum initially induced Ashkome to leave his Ashanapwan clan and the Mongeimbit men's house, and attempted to establish their friendship, indeed their brotherhood, with the gift of his son, Wankala, in adoption. Ashkome then brought his brother Mandjinakwon into his new clan and then adopted Taukumbank as his new brother and clansman. These latter two had loyalties to Ashkome as their sponsor but none to Tanum. Moreover, Ashkome was then able to subvert the loyalties of some of Tanum's own clansmen by patronizing them with the new European valuables provided him by his migrant relatives, including Mandjinakwon. Not surprisingly, the unity between Ashkome and Tanum was replaced by enmity as Ashkome transformed himself from ally to competitor. Tanum was hard pressed by Ashkome to remain in control of their clan. He was, in fact, accused in debates at this time of having retained importance only through the financial help he received through his association with Mead and Fortune.[7] (See Gewertz, 1983: 176–185).

It is likely, therefore, that the controversy focusing on the wife of Mandjinakwon was part of the continuing political struggle between Ashkome and Tanum. Indeed, those few alive during Deborah's fieldwork with knowledge of the events of the "Deja vue repeat quarrel" – including Wenente, the still lucid wife of Mandjinakwon, and two of Tanum's sons – agree. They told Deborah that the issue in the quarrel was part of a continuing struggle between

Ashkome and Tanum to achieve preeminence within their Monge-mali patriclan.

This conclusion well fits the data. For instance, Walinakwon and Megudimi, who were of concern to Taukumbank for setting the precedent of wife stealing, were closely allied to Tanum – they were the children by the two previous marriages of his present wife – and were recognized as generally acting on Tanum's behalf. Megudimi, it will be remembered, had gone up to the "house married," ostensibly acting on behalf of the bride's family, but after his visit the girl ran away to marry Walinakwon. Since Tanum had been successful with this form of attack, it would not be surprising if his next offensive was similar.

Taukumbank's "deja vue" makes additional sense when the relationship between Tanum and Kashibonga is considered. Kashi-bonga, the man who replaced Megudimi in Taukumbank's mind as a threat, is only distantly related to Wenente, the wife of Mandjinak-won. He is the sister's son of her former co-wife's husband. His relationship to Tanum, who was his sister's husband, is, however, much more direct. Could Taukumbank have been afraid, thus, that Kashibonga, like Megudimi before him, was about to convince a wife of Mandjinakwon to leave the side of Ashkome for that of Tanum? But why exactly should the competition between Ashkome and Tanum take this form: what is the cultural meaning for the Chambri of inducing a woman to leave one man for another?

Women and the theft of names

A man who loses his wife finds himself in great peril. Among the Chambri (as is frequently the case in tribal societies) a wife may be feared by her husband because she has access to such of his exuviae as hair clippings, nail pairings, sweat, saliva and semen. For these to be used effectively in Chambri sorcery, a man must first be weakened through the loss of his secret names. However, a wife is also in a good position to learn the secret names possessed by her husband, since he is likely to mutter them while asleep and dreaming about his ancestors. Although Chambri do not believe any woman has sufficient power to use the exuviae or names directly, they do regard her as capable of transmitting these to other men, usually to a father, brother or lover.

Taukumbank may have feared not only that his clansman, Mandjinakwon, was in danger, but that the other men of the clan, including himself, were threatened. Whatever names the wife of Mandjinakwon had learned were clan names; moreover, because she and Ashkome lived in the same house, she may well have acquired his exuviae along with those exceptionally powerful names which made him an important man. Taukumbank may have been especially concerned that Ashkome maintain his power because of his own dependence on him, but his response to the interest shown in the wife of Mandjinakwon shows also a typically male Chambri sense of vulnerability.

To still further complicate this analysis, Chambri men welcome attack at the same time they fear it. A man will, for instance, present his names as worth stealing and derive social verification as a man of power from the efforts of others to acquire them. The danger, of course, is that if a man's names are generally regarded as having been stolen, his identity and his capacity to resist attacks of sorcery are thought to be diminished. Understandably Taukumbank, Ashkome and their fellow clansmen were gratified as well as alarmed by Tanum's interest in the wife of Mandjinakwon.

Debates in the men's house frequently reflect this male dilemma of wishing to be sufficiently impressive that others attack and yet fearing the attack because it may be successful. Rhetoric characteristically oscillates between braggadocio and at least a pretense of humility. Thus, it would be perfectly possible for Michael Kubusa to deny, as he did during the Francis Yaboli debate described in Chapter 2, that his father had provided him with any secret powers and still in other debates boast that his names had brought Deborah to Chambri Island, or had deterred the *kiap* from collecting head taxes.

For comparable reasons it is also common to hear men shouting as they walk through a Chambri village about their loss through theft of an object of potentially exceptional power. A man might complain, for example, that a piece of wood he was transforming into a totemic effigy had been stolen before he had ritually empowered it. In this way he is suggesting that he is powerful enough to have enemies who wish to thwart him and, at the same time, hinting at the extent of his esoteric competence by reference to the scope of his plans. Yet he is also acknowledging that he has not, in fact, actually completed this wonderful object.

Women have a special place in this world where Chambri men must convince others of their importance through inviting and advertising attack. Although a man might brag that an object had been stolen from him, he would never brag that his wife had been stolen. Unlike women, objects are not greatly coveted since they do not themselves speak nor do they recognize and respond to the power of others. A man may, with little concern, leave a ritual object unattended in his wife's house until he needs it for a ceremony.[8] His wife or wives, however, can not themselves so safely be left unattended in the presence of outsiders who may wish to deprive him of his secret names. If a wife leaves for another, she carries with her the knowledge which his enemies can use to make him weaker than they. Moreover, the fact that his wife has left establishes that he has already become weaker than his enemies since their powers to attract are demonstrably stronger than his are to hold.

Male secrets and the attraction of women

It is within this context of male competition through inducing wives to leave husbands that we should examine Mead's view that Chambri women initiate sexual liaison and marriage. Consider, for example, the following excerpt from a (signed) love letter written in English by a 19-year-old Chambri man:

My Dearest Darling,
    I would like to inform you and give you advisement. This goes like that whenever I go to the market place you look at me myself too and you look enjoyable face maybe you love me I think that. Darling if it true please write a note to me and I will know all about it. While now on I don't write any single letter to any girls for three villages to be friends with me. This my first to write to you if you wish my letter, "if not forget about that." I just asking to be friend with me. . . .

This young man had noticed a young woman looking at him wherever they met. He decided to correspond with her, not to announce his fascination with her, but to provide her with an opportunity to acknowledge his power to attract her. If she was, indeed, overcome by his power, then she was invited to respond with a note of her own.

Both men and women believe that when a woman approaches a man with glances, letter, or small gifts it is because his totemic powers compel her to do so.[9] The young Chambri man who wrote the love letter was not expected to have as yet an identity of particular power and would not, therefore, be greatly concerned if the young lady failed to affirm her attraction to him. A powerful man like Ashkome, however, would be profoundly disturbed to have relinquished a wife or sister-in-law to a rival leader since it would indicate not that he was about to lose his power, but that he already had lost it. However, since the wife of Mandjinakwon had, on this occasion, remained, it was in the interests of Ashkome, Taukumbank and the others of their faction to claim that Tanum had made an attempt to induce her to leave. They could in this way advertise that their secrets were both valuable and safe and that their power to retain the wife of Mandjinakwon was greater than that of Tanum to attract her.

Ashkome could also be regarded as proclaiming a triumph when he asked the assembled participants: "Who was enough to pay back all he had paid for her?" Mead implies that this question was asked by a harried man who was embarrassed about the quarrel and wished it over as soon as possible. However, contemporary Chambri, again including Wenente and Tanum's sons, suggested that Ashkome was indeed delighted to have Tanum implicated in what had begun as a rather ordinary domestic dispute between co-resident women, and that his question about bride-price payments was more a brag than an effort at conciliation. By asking this question, he was asserting that no one would be able to pay back what he had paid for Wenente – certainly not Tanum. For it was Ashkome, not Tanum, who possessed the power to keep the woman as well as the power to acquire the valuables necessary to pay a large bride-price: these were the secrets, he implied, that Tanum coveted and hoped to acquire through stealing away the woman who might have learned them.

Chambri men must brag and swagger if they are to compete in a milieu where to fail to demonstrate fully that they have power would be to lose that power.[10] Unfortunately for them, as we shall also see, their swagger may do more to assert control over their women than to effect that control.

Male vulnerability and the power of women

In most cases, Chambri women would prefer not to be caught up in these male political intrigues. Wenente, for example, was much more concerned about her domestic relationships – preferring the company of her former co-wife to that of the woman whose house she now shared – than she was in the struggle for power between Ashkome and Tanum. However, when women do become the focus of male competition, their capacity to affect the fortunes of men does give them some actual power.

The recognition by men that women can bring about their ruin is, we think, reflected in a statement made to Mead by one of her male informants, a statement in which she locates a "contradiction at the root of Tchambuli society" (1935: 263). Mead reports this statement in the context of her discussion of whether Chambri women knew male ritual secrets.

The elaborate ceremonies, the beating of water-drums, the blowing of flutes, are no secrets from the women. As they stood, an appreciative audience, listening solemnly to the voice of the crocodile, I asked them: "Do you know what makes that noise?" "Of course, it is a water-drum, but we don't say we know for fear the men would be ashamed." And the young men answer, when asked if the women know their secrets: "Yes, they know them, but they are good and pretend not to, for fear we become ashamed. Also – we might become so ashamed that we would beat them."

"We might be so ashamed that we would beat them." In that sentence lies the contradiction at the root of Tchambuli society, in which men are theoretically, legally dominant, but in which they play an emotionally subservient role, dependent upon the security given them by women, and even in sex-activity looking to women to give the leads. (Ibid.)

That there are men manipulating water-drums in order to produce the crocodile-like sounds important during male initiation ceremonies is, as Mead correctly states, no surprise to any Chambri woman. Why, after all, should the relationships between men, their art objects, and their totems be a secret in this society which, as we have seen, is appropriately characterized by Bateson as producing an art of "immanent totemism . . . where the crocodiles, weevils, and ancestors with noble noses depicted on objects such as water drums, are the people who made them and the people who admired them" (1946:120)? Women understand, as well, that it is the totemic names which effect the union between man, water-drum and ancestral crocodiles and which give all of these their power. Women, indeed, know as much about the general characteristics of this immanent totemism as do their husbands since they too are recipients of totemic names and (some) objects of totemic significance.

Moreover, Chambri women understand how ritual objects are fashioned. Those few which are, in fact, hidden from women are concealed to protect them from female secretions which might pollute them, not to keep them secret.[11] Indeed, during a specific phase of male initiation, Chambri (as well as Iatmul) women are frequently shown those particular sacred flutes ordinarily kept from them.[12]

What then could any woman reveal that would make a man sufficiently ashamed so that he would beat her in retribution? Only if a *wife* were to proclaim that her husband's crocodile-voice is merely a water-drum – only if she were to declare him incapable of transmogrifying the water-drum into the ancestral crocodile, or himself into his ancestors – could a woman so shame a man. She alone could so reveal him as a man without powers, as a man who is, therefore, vulnerable to his enemies. He might, as Mead suggests, attempt to regain his lost prestige by demonstrating his power to beat her.

However, such an attempt to salvage his reputation is likely to be fruitless. Certainly if she persists in this denunciation of him, his enemies will seize upon her account as public verification of his weakness. Thus, Mead is correct when she suggests that Chambri men recognize that their security depends upon women: the security, however, stems less from the emotional support women may provide than for their women remaining politically disengaged.[13]

Women can, if they choose, thus act as political catalysts.[14] Indeed, we know of a case – truly a Chambri man's nightmare – in which a wife brought about her husband's suicide. The victim had been experiencing social difficulties for some time. His patriclan was particularly small and weak and had been unable to acquire sufficient valuables to compensate its affines. His wife, in addition, was rumored to have been seen in the company of another man, and everyone assumed that she had taken him as lover and would soon be leaving her husband to marry him. Certainly her brother had long encouraged her to leave her husband because of his incompetence as an affine. During one men's house debate when this potential realignment was mentioned, the distraught husband stood up to defend himself, only to trip and fall as he approached the orator's stool. All of these events were frequently discussed by his co-villagers, with a mixture of sorrow and derision.

Then his dog died. Within a few hours its putrescent carcass was buzzing with flies as it lay underneath the house of this man and his wife. The husband asked his wife to remove it and she shouted her refusal, offering no excuse other than her distaste for the job. The next day the request was repeated, and she again publicly refused. The following day, when she returned to her house with her catch of fish late in the afternoon, she found him dead, hanging from the rafters. He had become, everyone agreed, weak – too weak to be able to induce his wife to perform legitimate, though in this case distasteful, domestic tasks. Clearly, they thought, he had lost all of his powers and would soon succumb to sorcery.[15] The sorcery, Deborah was told, probably would come as retaliation from Iatmul living on the nearby Timbunmeri Island where his father had once seduced a woman.

Men are perhaps most clearly aware of their vulnerability to the initiatives of women when a married clansman dies. Mead recognizes in *Sex and Temperament* that a widow who is still young poses a particular threat, but, again, explains this fact in terms of a Western cultural preoccupation with the power of sexuality rather than in terms of a Chambri cultural preoccupation with totemic power and its potential loss. Mead writes:

With a young widow also, it is the girl's choice that is decisive, for men will not be foolish enough to pay for a girl who had not indicated her choice of husband by sleeping with him. It will be, as they say, money thrown away. A young widow is a tremendous liability to a community. No one expects her to remain quiet until her marriage has been arranged. Has she not a vulva? they ask. This is the comment that is continually made in Tchambuli: Are women passive sexless creatures who can be expected to wait upon the dilly-dallying of formal considerations of bride-price? Men, not so urgently sexed, may be expected to submit themselves to the discipline of a due order and precedence. (1935: 259)

It is true, as Mead argues, that women have little interest in due "order and precedence" and in the "dilly-dallying of formal considerations of bride-price." The reason, however, is not because of the strength of their sexual drives. Rather, they recognize that generating debts and credits through affinal exchange will not redeem them from debt.

Moreover, we argue, a widow is not regarded as a tremendous liability to the community because, as Mead implies, she knows more about sex and is, therefore, more likely to "sleep around." Rather, she is a liability because her knowledge of totemic names may lead her to "speak around." It is because a widow knows about the totemic names of the patriclan into which she has married, and because she might carry those names into another patriclan upon her remarriage that she is of concern, at least to the agnates of her dead husband. This concern is additionally great because the death itself suggests both that the clan is under attack and that its totemic powers have already been weakened. Under these conditions of increased vulnerability, a clan will be particularly concerned to keep its wives under control. Thus it becomes clear why men – even though they prefer to "marry around," and thereby generate the debts and credits through which they gain the opportunity to establish their worth – nonetheless find it very important that a classificatory brother marry the widow of a dead kinsman.

A widow who is young is, indeed, especially threatening, but this is because she has children yet to bear and is, for that reason, reproductively less committed to the clan of her deceased husband than is an older women. She is, therefore, regarded as particularly likely to form a new alliance. However, the threat to male interests a young widow poses by "speaking around" is mirrored in only somewhat attenuated form by the capacity of any widow or married woman to reveal secrets or in other ways play upon male vulnerability.

The strategies of a woman are in most cases, however, sufficiently distinct from those of her husband to make her largely indifferent to his political activities. Consequently, she does not necessarily object, or even much notice, when she becomes the focus of male intrigue. Moreover, her indifference to the machinations of competing males would usually be interpreted by her husband as satisfactory evidence of his totemic power to ensure her loyalty. When male concerns do directly affect her, as in the case of remarriage, men will be afraid to force her to adopt their concerns as hers. (See Errington and Gewertz, 1987a.) Men must accommodate themselves to her wishes, for as a discontented wife, she is likely to steal her husband's secrets and give them to a lover of her choice. Virtually any woman can in this way protect herself from what she interprets as an undue infringement upon her rights by her husband and his agnates.

Chapter 6
The mutual dependence of brothers and sisters

Although in their competition with each other, men often fear their wives, they rarely fear their sisters. Brothers and sisters (both actual and classificatory) are best able to pursue their respective interests if they can rely on the help of the other.[1] A sister's reproductive concerns will be advanced if her brothers can provide support for her and her children. In turn, a brother's political aspirations will be furthered if he receives assistance from his sisters and their children, particularly from the son toward whom he acts as *wau*.[2] In comparable fashion, brothers and sisters become bound to their mothers and mothers' brothers in such a manner that their own lives and the lives of their matrilateral kin become enmeshed.

On those occasions such as marriage and death which affect the entire clan, all male and female agnates, with the possible exception of the clan leader or leaders, present themselves as "brothers and sisters of the clan." Very important senior males may define themselves not as "brothers" but as "fathers" and in this role may choose either to direct or to remain aloof. Women, in contrast to the more competitive males, are much more likely to accept the interests of other members of their gender as their own. Certainly, relative seniority never prevents a woman from participating with other women of her clan.

Whether supporting a particular member of a clan or the clan as a whole, the differences in their respective strategies frequently lead men and women to act as brothers and sisters in separate ways. Sisters, in our first example, including the sisters of the clan (and those tied to the clan through women – the matrilateral kin), responded to the death by sorcery of 26-year-old Tadeos Kambukwat (whose funeral is about to be described) primarily as a personal loss which ruptured an important relationship of support. Brothers,

83

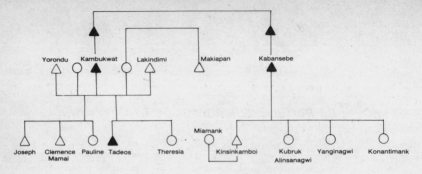

Figure 4.   A Genealogy of the Minginor Clan

including the brothers of the clan, regarded his death primarily as a matter affecting the distribution of power within and among clans.

Deborah's research assistant, Joseph Kambukwat, was Tadeos' younger half-brother. Born of different women, the two young men had not lived together in the same household since shortly after their father, Kambukwat, had died some 10 years before when they were still teenagers. Tadeos had then followed his mother to Kwalumem-bank clan land where her new husband, Lakindimi, lived; and Joseph had followed his mother to Yambai clan land where her new husband, Yorondu, lived.[3] The boys grew up as members of Kambukwat's Minginor clan but by the time they had become adults this clan had greatly declined in power.

The death of Tadeos placed the clan in serious jeopardy. As a young man, Joseph would not be able to establish himself as the leader of a viable clan without help, and, unfortunately, he could not expect effective support from other male agnates. His full brother, Clemence Mamai, for instance, would be of small help: as a permanent resident in the town of Wewak, this young man showed little interest in village politics. The only other adult male in the clan was Kinsinkamboi, the son of his father's parallel cousin, who was neither powerful nor particularly well disposed toward Kambu-kwat's sons.[4] With this death, everyone recognized that Minginor would amost certainly have to relinquish control over its remaining personnel, names and powers to another clan. (See Figure 4 for a geneaology of the Minginor clan.)

The funeral for Tadeos began at the house of Lakindimi. While Kinsinkamboi stood by watching, Tadeos' mother and her two sisters, together with his full sister, mourned over the body as it lay

Photograph 3.   Women mourn over Tadeos' corpse

in an open coffin on the floor. They crawled over the corpse, often lying on or massaging it. Then they began to dress the body in new clothes in preparation for burial by the Catholic Father the next day.[5] When Kambukwat's sister arrived, the women began crawling through the legs of each other: father's sister through mother's legs; sister through mother's legs.[6] Then they began to sing their dirges. They sang of the deceased Kambukwat, of his totems and his ancestors, as they continued to massage the body of his dead son, Tadeos. As Tadeos' mother sang, she banged her head against a wooden chair until a large welt appeared on her forehead. While singing of her dead patrikinsman, his sister touched Tadeos' immobile face and then brought her cupped hand to his mouth, gathering what was left of his breath into herself.[7] Lakindimi, the man with whom Tadeos had lived but who was not his kinsman, sat with a towel over his head in a corner of the house, muttering his own protective clan names. He lifted his head only once, to see the wife of Tadeos' mother's brother spill the milk of a coconut over the dead man's face. She had been sent by her husband, Makiapan, with the coconut, and with rice and fish, to feed Tadeos on behalf of his *wau* for the last time. Makiapan had been so overcome by grief that he was unable at first to attend.

The sisters, together with the clan's matrilateral supporters, continued their laments, until Patrick Yarapat arrived with Joseph to announce that the funeral would resume the following week, in more elaborate form, at Yarapat's spacious house. At this point those in attendance suddenly realized that Joseph had decided, probably without consultation with Kinsinkamboi, to seek the support and become the follower of the more powerful Yarapat. Moreover, Yarapat's interest in the death of Tadeos suggested that he was attempting to subsume the entire Minginor clan into his own Mangemeri clan. When Yarapat arrived with Joseph to move the funeral to his own house, he was asserting, with Joseph's compliance, that the concerns of the Minginor clan were the same as those of his Mangemeri clan, as well as demonstrating that his own power was sufficient to sponsor an impressive ceremony.

Ceremony for the dead at Yarapat's house

The funeral proceedings at Yarapat's house were the most elaborate ritual event that Deborah had ever witnessed on Chambri Island. Indeed, this funeral ritual was so elaborate that it had not been staged for over 40 years. While preparations were under way, Yarapat announced that he had decided to resurrect this ceremony in order to "teach all of our children about ancestral customs, as Prime Minister Michael Somare, our Sepik compatriot, has instructed us to do."[8] As a cultural revival, Yarapat's funeral was not only a nationalist message at a time when independence from Australia was imminent; it was also a demonstration that he could establish access to an avenue of power long closed to other Chambri. We have available a description of this funeral by Kenneth Gewertz, whose following account well conveys the immediate impression it created on a Western observer:

It was just after dark when we arrived at Yarapat's. There were so many people outside milling around the entrance, ascending and descending the long, carved entrance ladder, and so much noise, that I got the impression of a crowded nightclub during showtime. This impression was enhanced by the sound of singing, flute music, and a beating of the *kundu* [hand drum]. The drum was keeping a slow, 4/4 rhythm, which sounded not unlike a jazz or blues beat. When I climbed the ladder and looked inside, my impression changed. "A Christmas party," I thought. In the center of

Yarapat's large house, there stood what looked like an enormous, decorated tree. It went nearly to the ceiling and was at least eight feet in diameter. The house was full of people. All three villages seemed to be there. They sat on the floor, walked about, stood near the walls. I was glad that Yarapat's house was so solidly built. I didn't think that an ordinary house could take the strain. Then I noticed that the enormous tree was not standing, after all, but swinging. It was suspended by two *kanda* [rattan] fastenings to the great roof beam. As I watched, it slowly approached, then receded, then approached again. It was not a tree ... but a framework entirely covered by sprigs from different kinds of palm. Leaves from other trees were stuck in also. Hanging from this structure were *bilums* [net bags] bulging with what I later learned was food for the dead, and suits of clothing, pants and shirts, cleaned and neatly ironed, suspended on hangers from the leafy mass. [All of these were donated by the "sisters of the clan" who in this context of political incorporation were women of both Minginor and Mangemeri.] I realized that this must be the bed we had heard about. As the huge enclosure swung back and forth, I heard rippling flute music. I looked around for the players, but was unable to find them. "Man i winim mambu em i we" [Where are the the the flute players], I asked Joseph Kambukwat. "Em i stap insait." [They are inside.] I passed on to the other side of the bed. There a table was set up. It was covered with decorative leaves. There was also a "money tree" ... but a small one with only a few dollar bills on it. [This was destined for Makiapan, Tadeos' mother's brother, in return for having provided Tadeos with his last "meal".] Illumination was provided by kerosene lamps, which were present in great numbers all over the house. Behind the table sat the musicians. To return to the nightclub comparison, they seemed very much like a group of jazz musicians performing for a noisy inattentive audience, but doing their enthusiastic best all the same. The musicians were Kinsinkamboi, Moses Angi, Kandank, Yorondu, Yarapat and Thomas Yankiman. Each had a chair, but preferred, at times, to stand while performing. Yankiman and Kandank kept time by beating with pieces of split bamboo. The rest played *kundus*. They sang with pleasure and abandon I had not seen before. Yorondu especially seemed gratified by this opportunity to perform. At times they all sang in unison; at other times they took choruses in succession. During the slower, sadder songs, they seemed to rival each other to see who could produce the thinnest, most pained and faltering voice. Kandank, I would say, emerged victorious here. Lying back in his chair, his eyes closed, he looked as though he had fallen into agonizing sleep. When his turn came, however, a pitiable creak emerged from his laboring lips which he managed to sustain until the end of the verse. While these gentlemen were performing, several old women, sisters of the clan, carried on a performance of their own. Each naked to the waist and decorated with markings in white clay, they seemed to function as caretakers of the swinging bed. Every so often, one or two of them would walk around the bed and replace pieces of palm frond which the swinging motion had caused to fall. At other times one of them would walk around it with a glowing piece of wood, dousing the leaves with smoke as with a censer. The old women would also dance. For this purpose they would take up a sprig of leaves which they would then wave back and forth, saluting the bed, as they rocked their bodies in time to the music. At other times they would stand facing the musicians, their backs to the bed. At one point two women were stationed in this fashion, like a pair of ancient go-go dancers. One was especially notable. Between the wrinkled, empty bladders of her breasts, she wore a huge metal cross and, as she swayed back and forth, making the shiny pendant swing and joggle in the dim light, she puffed vigorously on a handmade cigarette. Meanwhile, somewhere unnoticed by me, a pig was being roasted and cut into little squares, rice was being simmered, coffee was brewed, and *saksak* [sago] pancakes were prepared. These began to emerge as the *kundu*-playing singers continued to perform in alternation with the flautists inside the bed. Yarapat and Elaminakwon [Yarapat's Mangemeri agnate] began their judicious distribution of these refreshments ... [At the same time the sisters of the clan were beginning another set of activities. Before dawn they had cut the hair of Tadeos' agnates, his clan brothers who now included Yarapat, provided them with new clothes and decorations, and prepared the totemically significant floral arrangement which they would bury in the water at the end of the ceremony. This would complete the conversion of Tadeos into an ancestor.]

The concerns expressed by the brothers and sisters of the clan Minginor/Mangemeri during the modest lamentation at Lakindimi's house and during the lavish funeral display at Yarapat's house were largely the same. However, at Yarapat's house, the separate interests of each became crystallized. As Tadeos was transformed from corpse into ancestor under Yarapat's direction, the women grieved with ritualized anguish over the loss of their clan brother; the men became engrossed with the political significance of the occasion for intra- as well as inter-clan relationships. Moreover, by employing a form of ritual that defined the participants not only in terms of their clan but, also, their patrimoiety affiliation, Yarapat was asserting that this occasion was of significance for the entire society.

Although, as we have seen, specific totemic powers are owned and employed by the members of a particular clan, there are, in addition, certain ritual apparatus, techniques and knowledge that belong to and are used by the moiety as a collectivity. Thus, when Yarapat chose to include the flutes, which were in fact the property of his moiety, as a central part of the funeral for Tadeos, he was inviting his entire moiety to participate. Moreover, since the moieties are ideally exogamous and, hence, regarded as affinally related, the activities of one moiety are supposed to engage the attentions of the other. Only someone as wealthy as Yarapat could afford the expenses – including presentations of food and valuables – of a ritual which involved so many members of Chambri society.

We begin our analysis of the transformation of Tadeos, and the delineation of the concerns of the brothers and sisters thus effected, by focusing on the mysterious flutes. Hidden within the bed – the *sabulintoub* – these flutes made Tadeos into an ancestor and, as we will see, at the same time, played an essential part in the process which transformed Minginor clan into Yarapat's Mangemeri clan. Significantly, the Chambri think that these powerful flutes are sisters crying for their dead brothers. According to Chambri myth, these flutes were acquired by an ancestor named Sengabi.

The acquisition of the flutes

Sengabi, the most peripatetic of Chambri ancestors, is credited by his descendants with many accomplishments, including the formation of fish-for-sago barter markets throughout the Sepik. He is said to have persuaded the Mensuat to exchange their sago for Chambri fish; to have established a market between the fish-producing Iatmul of Nyaurengai, Korogo and Kandingai and the sago-supplying Sawos of Torembi; and to have persuaded the people of the bush near Wagu to exchange their sago for Yambon fish. Moreover, he is thought to have traveled as far as Wewak, teaching those he met that to remain strong – literally, to be able to "sit in your own house, supported by your own central post" – they must recognize not only their economic but their cultural interdependence with the other groups of their area.

Indeed, on one of his trips he set out to find flutes which would match the Amakio flutes used by those of the patrimoiety, *nyeminimba*, to mourn for their clan dead. Sengabi, as a member of the opposite patrimoiety, *nyauinimba*, had been denied the use of these and so, shortly after the death of an agnate, he went forth in search of flutes appropriate for those of his own moiety. He traveled among the Sawos, carrying with him a huge sleeping bag woven by his sister, and large enough to protect many families from the bloody depredations of ferocious Sepik mosquitos. The Sawos men from

Nogosop and Gaikerobi wished to acquire the mosquito bag with many *kina*, *lin* and *talimbun*, but when Sengabi heard the distant sound of the flutes known as Lokwi, he asked for and was given these instead. Accompanied by two Sawos flutists who were to instruct the men of his *nyauinimba* moiety, Sengabi brought these flutes home.

The Chambri interest in the flutes of their neighbors must be seen as part of a general preoccupation of Middle Sepik people with exchanging their cultural products. Consider, for example, one of the notes Bateson provided about the collection of Sepik artifacts housed at the Museum of the Faculty of Archaeology and Anthropology at Cambridge University.

These [four heads of supernatural beings, made of hollow and open ended basket-work] were collected by me in Tshuosh [Sawos] territory and taken to Kankanamun village, where the natives were much impressed by them and identified them as *wagan nambu* (i.e. wagan "heads"). Among the Iatmul *wagan nambu* are very sacred objects ... They are not worn as masks. Probably these objects are not *wagan nambu*, or among the Tshuosh *wagan nambu* are held in very much less respect and reverence than among the Iatmul ...

In the American Museum of Natural History, New York, there is a pair of basketwork heads almost identical with these. Those specimens were collected by Dr Mead in Chambuli and she believes that they were made there. If that is correct, it is possible that these Cambridge specimens were looted from Chambuli. (1962:9)

Because of their extensive trade in ceremonial masks, artifacts, and dance complexes, the people of this region were described by Mead as having an "importing culture" (1970: 178–206). One possible explanation for this predilection to borrow, as it appears among the Chambri, is suggested by that aspect of their cosmology which posits the dispersal of totemic powers with each new generation. In such a universe, the infusion of exogenous totemic secrets into the repertoire of a clan would be revitalizing.

Regardless of whether the *wagan* heads were looted from Chambri, or traded by Chambri – or whether the Sawos used the heads as masks or as items of display – these objects could all have been valued by the Chambri and, we suspect, by their neighbors, as at least a potential source of power. Moreover, since Chambri think that it takes power to "pull" powerful objects to Chambri, they, at least, would regard these infusions of power as reinforcing, rather than disrupting, the existing distribution of power.

Indeed, where power is finite and forever dispersing, unless "importing" is pursued with some vigor, the "central post" will lose its strength to sustain each of these groups as intact and autonomous.[9] Thus, if the Sawos had acquired their *wagan* heads from the Chambri, Chambri could well have acquired their powerful Lokwi flutes from the Sawos. The power of the Lokwi flutes was, indeed, apparent once Sengabi and his party arrived home. There they found that the funeral bed had already been built for Sengabi's dead agnate. Since no one was nearby, the two Sawos flutists were able to enter the bed's leafy enclosure unobserved. When members of the family of the deceased did arrive, they were happy because they then heard in the sound of the flutes the voices of the ancestral sisters lamenting a brother's death.

The flutists inside the bed at Yarapat's house spoke, in a similar way, with the voices of Tadeos' ancestral sisters. They recited the esoteric names that are part of the store of knowledge of his *nyauinimba* patrimoiety, including the names of Tukwananimbil, the *nyauinimba* mother of Yako, the moon, and the territories the two inhabited.[10] At the same time, the men seated in front of the bed were playing their drums and singing the exoteric names of these same characters and places, as well as of their activities. Their songs were of the grief and concern that the members of their *nyauinimba* moiety were experiencing.[11] Thus, they sang of Tukwananimbil's worry over her son as he illuminated the patch of *kunai* grass on Chambri Island called Silunakwan – and of Yako's response, thanking his mother for her concern and for the work she had undertaken over the years on his behalf; they sang again of Tukwananimbil, who wept as she watched Yako's moonbeams swallowed by the undulations of Chambri Lake.[12]

To bring ancestral voices into the realm of the living and in this way establish a channel to ancestral power is, in the Chambri view, the essential purpose of ritual knowledge. Through a revival, which was virtually a reimportation, of this ceremony, Yarapat was acting as a contemporary Sengabi: he was bringing power into Chambri life in a dramatic and compelling demonstration of his capacity to negate entropy.[13] (Yarapat's show of power prompted one of his disgruntled competitors to complain to Deborah after this ceremony that "Yarapat with his big house and lavish ceremonies was acting just like God.") However, the Lokwi flutes were not only ancestral voices, they were the voices of ancestral sisters; they not only mourned Tadeos, they also transformed him.

Sisters as transformers

Clan sisters – the female agnates – assume the role of transformer in all major rites of passage for Chambri males. At the birth of a clansman, they assist the mother in delivery and help establish the child as a member of their clan by planting totemically significant flora and by giving him totemically significant names which, although not esoteric, denote him as a member of their particular clan. Later, at the time of his initiation, clan sisters again participate: After the cuts an initiate has received on his back and legs have largely healed – these cuts are supposed to release some of the blood internalized from his mother during his gestation – he emerges from seclusion and the sisters of the clan give birth to him as an adult member of their clan. They do this by first washing away the paint he has worn as a novice with water they carry in *talimbun* – described in Chapter 4 as wombs – and then by feeding him.[14] And finally at his death they prepare his corpse for burial and at the conclusion of their mourning – at the conclusion of their relationship with him as a member of the living – they plant the same sorts of totemically significant flora which had marked his birth. In these, and in other ways such as at a boy's first haircutting, the sisters of the clan claim him as their social child.[15]

This capacity of sisters to transform brothers is exemplified in an important myth about the first Chambri ship-builder, Arione, who is credited with teaching Europeans to construct all of their sophisticated conveyances, including airplanes. (See Errington and Gewertz, 1985, for a complete account of this myth). Significantly, the ship which carried Arione to Australia and beyond and the bed which conveyed Tadeos to the realm of the ancestors were each "empowered" by sisters.

The circumstances of Arione's birth were unusual. He was born from a female snake who had consumed the semen spilled by a man while making love to his wife in their garden. Shortly after his birth, this man and his wife brought Arione into their family as brother to their two daughters. They did not tell him of his biological mother, and one day he accidentally killed the snake while cutting grass. Informed then that the snake was his mother, Arione at first grieved mightily, carrying the snake's bones around his neck in a palm-bark basket, and refusing all food and drink. Eventually, he agreed to eat the sago and other foods his two sisters brought him. "He ate what they brought, vomited, but then was all right. 'Now I'm a man,' he said." He was then able to build his boat.

After his boat was completed, he sang magic names which turned his sisters into part of the ship's motor. Once the ship began to move, Arione cried out other of his patrilineal and matrilateral names, and fully empowered his boat by turning the man and his wife into the rest of the motor. In this craft he traveled to distant places, teaching others to construct similar vessels.

Significantly, Arione became powerful enough to travel unharmed throughout the world, not by establishing his fundamental autonomy from his family, but by continuing to rely on them. In particular he relied on his sisters. By providing him with food, as sisters would do after a brother's scarification ceremony, they helped him to forget his biological snake mother and he was able to become a social adult.[16]

Thus, the sisters of Arione, like all sisters, have the vital ceremonial role of making their brothers over into strong agnates. As is most obvious during the ceremony of initiation, sisters create their brothers as strong clansmen through a social analog of birth which serves to attenuate, although by no means entirely to eradicate their connection with the clans of the women who bore them. When these brothers are dead, their sisters prepare them for burial and reiterate their patriclan membership through the planting of totemic flora; at the same time and in parallel fashion, the Lokwi sisters effect the passage which enables Tadeos and other of their dead brothers to emerge as ancestors.

Of sisters, mothers and mothers' brothers

Although *nyeminimba* is regarded to be as fully separate from *nyauinimba* as are their respective collective representations – meta-totems – of the moon/vulva and the sun, the two moieties are also considered perpetually linked.[17] Thus, the Lokwi flutes not only wailed with the concern that sisters express for the death of a brother, but wailed with the concern that Tukwananimbil, a mother, expressed for her son, Yako. Similarly, although a woman produces children for a patrilineal group not her own she never loses her connection to them, even after blood-letting of initiation, because they carry her blood.[18]

This tie of blood between a mother and child remains unbroken even in death, and provides a "road" through which the ancestors of the mother's clan maintain and express a wide range of concerns for the welfare of the living of the opposite moiety. A Chambri shaman will, for example, through "reading his or her blood" be able to receive advice from an ancestor of his or her mother's clan on how to resolve a difficulty.[19]

These bonds of blood also provide the link between mother's brothers and sister's children.[20] A mother's brother provides what is regarded as maternal support in the form of nurture for one of his sister's sons and so establishes a tie which becomes an important part of male political strategy.

Each Chambri man, in his competitive effort to achieve equality with those who produced him, must attempt to demonstrate his individual importance. His success requires not only that his clan be powerful but that he be distinguished from the other males of his clan as the most powerful. The link between a mother's brother and his designated sister's son allows each to differentiate himself from his agnates. As one of the few non-competitive relationships possible between Chambri men it enables an individual to find someone outside his clan whom he can trust and, moreover, an ally whom he does not share with his agnates. Within a patriclan, a senior man seeks the help of his sister's son in his efforts to control his juniors and, thus, retain clan leadership; conversely, a junior agnate seeks to evade the control of his seniors through recourse to his mother's brother.

Reo Fortune describes an argument between Tanum and two of his sons, Ndumunduma and Kundungwi, which indicates both the degree to which antagonism can be created between male agnates and the nature of the relationship between mother's brother and sister's son. As part of the continuing competition between Ashkome and Tanum over the control of their clan (see Chapter 5), Ashkome had provided Ndumunduma with Apong as wife. Tanum then retaliated against Ashkome and Ndumunduma by having intercourse with Apong; Kundungwi then attacked both his father and his brother by following suit (see Fortune, 1933a, and Gewertz, 1981: 175–186). Then each of the sons in this bitterly competitive display of sexual power sought help from his mother's brother. Fortune writes:

Kundungwi went to seek his waus in Kilimbit. Ndumunduma went to seek his waus in [the men's house] Boroboroman. [Each son having been born of a different wife.]

Yekeimali, one of the latter, leaving Ndumunduma in Boroboroman, arrived very annoyed and indignant ... Yekeimali addressed me seriously and worriedly, saying that he'd take Ndumunduma with him and they'd both go altogether and settle in Palimbei [Village] on the Sepik. (1933a)

Yekeimali, as Ndumunduma's *wau* had undoubtedly assumed personal responsibility for fulfilling all matrilateral obligations to Ndumunduma at his initiation, including making the first cut, and had endowed him with names and powers for use during his lifetime. What Yekeimali taught Ndumunduma would be his alone and would distinguish him from his patriclan brothers, including Kundungwi. He could use these matrilaterally bestowed powers as well as his relationship to Yekeimali to further and defend his own interests within his patriclan. Indeed, men so greatly value these matrilateral bequests that they not infrequently speak of their particular mothers' brothers as having taught them everything of importance.

Yekeimali's concern for Ndumunduma's welfare, moreover, was probably much stronger than any he might have had for his own sons or other junior agnates. Fathers do allocate some of their powers to their sons in order to indebt and empower them sufficiently so that they become effective supporters. However, since sons replace fathers within patriclans, to the extent a senior male gives important names and powers to his junior agnates, he also fosters his own political eclipse. One could not, for instance, easily imagine Tanum relinquishing any of his real power to either of his sons at this time of intense political competition within their clan.[21] Nonetheless, a man would not wish to withhold his powers permanently from his clan since his viability as an ancestor depends on the ritual capacities of his living agnates.

Senior males find a solution to this dilemma in the relationship they have with their maternal nephews.[22] As we have seen, the powers a mother's brother gives to his sister's son in the form of names are legitimately alienated from the mother's brother's clan, but only during the life of the sister's son. Consequently, a man can, without fundamentally weakening his clan, ensure that his sons – and junior agnates more generally – are delayed in their access to ritual secrets which would make them more fully able to compete with him.

In a comparable way, a significant portion of a clan's valuables are not subject to immediate claim by junior male agnates. By endowing their daughters with clan valuables, fathers forestall rivalry with their sons. In a citation presented earlier about the marriage arrangements made for the child, Mariabiendwon, Mead noted:

the little girl, who is only about eleven ... being flashed by distant "brothers," Werebongo and Kaviwon. *The flash was provided by the girl's "Father,"* individual unit contributions also made by Monolable, Yapona-kin, and Mamandi ... *The flash, which is hung up intact in a bilum which went with it and which belongs to the girl will be given by her to her son*, was meagre and consisted of: a skull cap of netting with a few gams tied to it, 1 long string of native buttons, a string of 6 fat gams, 2 leglets of me, a lime gourd slightly flashed with me, 2 short strings of European buttons, a string of 20 sliced gams, a huge cut gam, 1 string of large old buttons, 3 ovalis shells. (1933, emphasis our own.)

These valuables provided to a daughter by her senior patrilateral kin in trust for her son will, in fact, eventually be used by him to compensate her brother. Mariabiendwon will give to her son, in other words, those valuables which he will use to begin repaying his affine, her particular brother who acts as his *wau*, for the fact of his existence. In this sense, a father's gift to his daughter is really a delayed bequest to his son.[23]

The delay of the gift will probably retard, or at least, inhibit the political ascent of the son: Fathers are likely to remain more important than their sons since much of the clan wealth they control is initially diverted from their own sons to their daughters' sons. Men receive portions of their patrimonies from their sisters' sons, when their fathers are likely to be already dead.

Yet a sister also provides her brother with the eventual opportunity to achieve equality with his father. Through her marriage she becomes the basis of the relationship of affinal inequality which will lead her husband and his clan to convey the valuables on which her brother's own marriage, affinal presentations and political hopes depend. Through her marriage she produces the son who will return her brother's patrimony to him, who will continue for the duration of her brother's life to give him physical and monetary support in the form of affinal presentations and services, and who will, in addition, proclaim him as a powerful and beneficent mother's brother.

Sisters help to transform their brothers into strong social adults and brothers support the interests of their sisters and sisters' children if these conflict with those of husbands and husbands' agnates.[24] The mutuality of their interests emerges almost inevitably: If it is their children who provide sisters with the opportunity of becoming persons of worth, it is sisters and their children – particularly their sons – who provide brothers with their chance to do the same.

Intersection of the interests of brothers and sisters

The strategies followed by both Chambri men and women to achieve worth are significantly shaped by the fact that women produce children for patriclans not their own. Because mother and child are of different clans, a woman must repay her ontological debts with progeny under the control of her husband's clan. That her interests reside in the prospects of her children does not, however, lead her to identify fully with her own husband and his clan. She, therefore, encourages her brother to recognize the blood he shares with her and her children and to extend his concern to them so that their fortunes – by which she defines herself– will not be completely in the hands of her husband and his agnates.[25] A husband, in his turn, fears his wife because he recognizes that she is not necessarily committed to his interests which are defined in terms of his clan. He, therefore, looks to his sisters who through acts of social birth replicate, and to some extent supersede, the ties of blood and concern between his wife and his children.

Yet the interests of brothers and sisters do not entirely converge for the reason that men, much more than women, find their opportunities to achieve worth inextricably linked with the fortunes of their clans. It is only as a member of a clan that a man can achieve sufficient power to become the equal of those who caused him. None of the social relationships of a man – as father, brother, uncle and nephew – truly divert his focus from his patriclan. Indeed, as we have seen, his matrilateral relationships in fact enable him to increase his political efficacy within his own clan. In contrast, because the social relationships of a woman – as sister, wife and mother – derive their unity from a focus on her children, a woman does not regard the preeminence of any particular clan as of ultimate concern.

Thus, when Yarapat built the *sabulintoub* in which Tadeos was transported to the ancestral world by his moiety sisters, the Lokwi flutes, and thereby assumed ceremonial responsibility for Minginor while demonstrating his own power, the men of the clan were affected in a substantially different way than were the women. For Minginor to be subsumed within Mangemeri was from the male perspective a major political realignment which would have extensive repercussions: Although men from both clans would benefit as members of a single more powerful clan, the competition among them for relative eminence within the clan would become stiffer.

Moreover, because Yarapat was a strong leader he would also be a formidable competitor. From the perspective of the sisters of the clan – of Joseph's sister, Pauline; of Tadeos' sister, Theresia; and of Kinsinkamboi's sisters, Konantimank, Yanginagwi and Kubruk Alinsanagwi – this relatively amicable takeover had a rather different significance.

Indeed, as we have seen, a woman would expect her children to prosper if her brothers could be members of a clan more powerful than Minginor. At the same time, however, as women wish their brothers to be strong and their clan to be powerful, they also regard much of the competition among men with misgivings: when a clan turns against itself as in the paroxysm of enmity between Tanum and his sons, or when sorcery is epidemic, women find their own objectives threatened.[26] Thus when the sisters of Minginor – indeed, the sisters of all patriclansmen – think of their brothers, they do so not altogether out of a direct concern that these brothers succeed as individuals in the male competition to acquire worth; rather, their preoccupation is likely to be on behalf of those who call these brothers *wau*. As Yanginagwi put it: "I cannot forget that Tadeos, my *masin* [younger brother], was *wau* to my sons and daughters." And when Konantimak, like an ancient go-go dancer, swayed back and forth in time to the music of the *kundus* at Tadeos' funeral, her thoughts, we suspect, were more upon Tadeos as the departed *wau* of Theresia's children than they were upon him as clan brother whose death meant that Minginor lost its political autonomy.

Chapter 7
Marriage and the confluence of interests

We have throughout this book emphasized the importance of marriage as providing an essential context in which men and women pursue their respective interests. We now examine the ritual that establishes marriage. In this ritual, the interests and strategies of men and women, as they encounter each other as husband, wife, brother and sister, are brought into immediate and clarifying juxtaposition. Moreover, through the intensification characteristic of ritual, they are depicted with particular precision. In the ceremony of marriage the Chambri elucidate for themselves the distinct concerns of men and women while demonstrating that these can be articulated to form a single social system.

Marriage: unity and opposition

During the evening of December 26, 1983, members of Pekur Sinsung's clan gathered in the house of his younger brother, Mundi, to raise money needed for the bride-price of Bibi Daisy Yambun, soon to be married to Theo Pekur, Pekur's eldest son. Pekur first laid a newly purchased sleeping mat on the floor of the house, where individuals were to place the money they wished to contribute to the bride-price. Then, so that he and his agnates would have an accurate record of how much had been paid by whom, a young mission-educated clansman was stationed nearby with a notebook to keep tally.[1] In the course of the evening, the considerable sum of just over $K1,642 was gathered. The major portion was presented by Pekur himself as his own contribution, although this was largely composed of monies earned by younger clansmen, including Theo, who worked in the towns.

While the men sat around the sleeping mat, presiding over the

99

Photograph 4.   The men sit around the sleeping mat, presiding over the accumulation of the bride-price

accumulation of the money donated by both men and women, the wives and the sisters of the clan were singing and dancing together in the remaining half of the house.[2] Their songs, composed of short phrases of totemic importance followed by chants of nonsense syllables, were derisive and produced shouts of laughter from both men and women. Thus, a wife would pretend to celebrate Mundi, one of the totemic names of Pekur's younger brother, by singing of her overwhelming desire to eat his head. A sister would ridicule Mandoi, a totemically significant rat of Pekur's clan, by accusing

Photograph 5. In their songs, wives and sisters express a fundamentally similar perspective

her clan brothers of their ratlike behavior in consuming what they stole without sharing the spoils. In these songs wives and sisters were expressing a fundamentally similar perspective toward the clan since the satirical support of the wives expressed much the same sentiment as did the mocking deprecation of the sisters.

In addition, wives and sisters frequently danced together with linked arms and legs to the refrains, regardless of who had initiated and devised the verse. As frequently, a wife or sister would stop her dancing to crawl through the legs of a sister or a wife, calling the woman, who had just "given birth" to her, "mother" and being called "daughter" in return, regardless of the kin ties they actually shared or their relative ages. So while Pekur and his kinsmen united as solidary wife-takers to accumulate the money necessary to acquire a woman from their wife-givers, their sisters and wives were uproariously ignoring not only the distinction of generation but the structural distinction between affines by describing themselves as merged daughter-mothers and mother-daughters. Even those clan sisters who contributed to the bride-price and who did derive a measure of status and prestige from the game of affinal exchange successfully played were thus discounting the importance of agnation and affinal opposition as the fundamental basis of identity.

But how could it have been otherwise? Since women produce children for a clan other than their own, they are unlikely to take with male seriousness the principle that clan identity generates absolute differences. Such differences, after all, would absolutely divide them from the children who, as we have argued, provide mothers with the chance of replacing themselves. The events of the following several days continued to demonstrate these differences in male and female perspective.

The next morning the sisters and wives of Pekur's clan, with other relatives and friends of the groom, left Mundi's house chanting exoteric names of Pekur's patriclan and moiety. They were on their way to present Bibi's father, Yambunapan, with the bride-price, necessary if they were to claim his daughter as bride. Leading their procession was the genealogically most senior male of Pekur's clan – in this case the eldest son of Pekur's father's eldest brother – whom Pekur and his agnates address as "father." At their destination, the group paused outside Yambunapan's house, while this "father" ascended the staircase alone to deliver the *bilum* containing the bride-price into Yambunapan's hands.[3]

Then, led by Theo Pekur's mother's brother, the sisters and wives of Pekur's clan twice approached and withdrew from the staircase, carrying a long rope designed to "hook" the girl and pull her to them. During this time the bride was seated just inside her father's house, facing the entrance. Bibi was dressed in an immaculate "laplap" and "meri blouse" with shell and feather accessories.[4] Seated next to her was her younger sister, also elaborately dressed as a potential bride, to indicate that there might well be future marriages between this and Pekur's clan. Both girls sat impassively although surrounded by mothers, mothers' sisters, father's sisters, brothers and fathers' brothers wailing the impending loss of their child. One maternal aunt, for example, began singing dirges for Bibi. A paternal aunt wailed that Bibi was about to abandon her father and mother to marry a stranger. And, as Theo Pekur's mother's brother and his entourage approached for the third and final attempt at hooking the bride, a paternal uncle cried out: "Oh, we're losing our daughter now."

Encouraged by shouts from his companions of "pull her," "hook her," "catch her," "bring her to us," Theo Pekur's mother's brother began to escort Bibi from her paternal home. Her mother and

Photograph 6. Bibi Yambunapan is introduced to an ancestral crocodile

maternal aunts threw themselves at her feet as if to block her path, but the affinal hook had already achieved a secure if metaphoric hold. Crying, "oh, mama, why are you leaving me so soon," Bibi's mother, upon seeing the last of her daughter as an unmarried woman, negated the generational differences between them.

As Bibi was led from Yambunapan's house back to Mundi's where the groom awaited, she was still accompanied by her sister and, in addition, by a clan brother who had been designated to convey her patrimony – a *bilum* containing $K100.00, eventually to go to her son. In the course of her transition Bibi was introduced to a series of powerful ancestral crocodiles: whenever she passed the site of a men's house – even where no men's house currently stood – Theo Pekur's mother's brother stopped the procession, had Bibi take a seat on the chair brought for the occasion, and proudly announced: "This woman has been married to a man of this village who is known and whose family has acted toward her family as correctly as anyone could have wished." Indeed, on this trip home, the entire party who had gone to fetch the bride participated in the triumph of Pekur's clan by joining in such songs as "We of the patrimoiety of *nyauinimba* have shot a woman," or "We who hold the territories of Perundui and Ambundui have won."

The celebration continued when the wedding party reached Mundi's house, although by this time the bride and groom had been sequestered to allow them time to be alone. On one of the few occasions that men and women perform together, the celebrators danced in unison and continued to sing the songs of Pekur's clan. Then a party of Bibi's patrilineal and matrilateral kin entered, carrying as display the bride-price just presented and, in addition, bringing the objects which conferred her maturity. One brought the clay hearth Bibi would use to fry sago; another, a suitcase full of clothes; yet another, a betel nut seedling. Still others of her kin provided the sleeping mat, the pots, pans, lamps, canoe paddles, and everything else she would use in her adult domestic life. And each gift was reciprocated by Pekur. With his hands full of $K2.00 notes, he circulated throughout the house and in the process of generously compensating each donor spent over $K150.00. Indeed, he even recompensed Yambunapan for the clothes and accessories Bibi was wearing that day of her wedding.

Then, when everyone was satisfied with the gifts given and repaid, Yambunapan's family engaged with Pekur's in the celebration. Although all the members of each group danced to the totemic chants of the other, it was the women who joined together with greatest enthusiasm. And of these, Pekur's sister and Bibi's mother, who had linked their arms and legs to hop together in time to the music, were particularly enjoying themselves. But, almost as if the high degree of solidarity now expressed by these women from inter-marrying patriclans threatened the centrifugal forces necessary to maintain the wife-givers as a group opposed to the wife-takers, Bibi's clan brother suddenly interrupted to remind Pekur's group of its responsibilities.

As he enumerated the obligations of his affines to the new bride, he ticked off each of his points by taking a coconut frond with his right hand from the bunch he held in his left.[5] His affines, he stated, must provide Bibi with a canoe, show her the betel nut trees she could harvest, show her the fishing grounds owned by her husband's clan and never chastize her for using property belonging to those whose children she will bear. In response, Pekur cheerfully accepted these obligations. And then, still in a joyful mood, Pekur berated those young girls who would marry non-Chambri men and deprive their parents of the pleasure of seeing them correctly wed.

But immediately he was informed by Bibi's clan brother that there was more to correct procedure than the exchange of valuables. Correctness means, he warned, that she must never be beaten after she visits her brothers. She must be asked first why she visited them: it must never be assumed that she did so in order to have an affair with one of her clan brothers, or was using the visit to her brothers to conceal an affair with someone else. The groom's younger brother then promptly countered by reminding Bibi's clan brother that the girl had been acquired at considerable cost. Because her family had accepted such a large bride-price, they had abdicated their right to interfere when she and her husband fought. Indeed, he continued, so high was the bride-price that her father and brothers had, in large measure, already been compensated if she were to be killed by her husband during a fight.[6]

A friend of the bride's family intervened by agreeing that the bride-price was, in fact, quite high. However, he added, the money that Bibi had brought with her – the $K100.00 placed in the *bilum* carried for her by her clan brother as she was introduced to the ancestral crocodiles – was to remain hers. It was her "pass book" – her bank account – and it must never be spent by anyone other than Bibi, certainly not by her new husband to buy beer.

Sensing that the oratory was escalating passions to such an extent that schism was threatened, a friend of the groom began to beat a drum to suggest the resumption of dancing, while another friend told the bride's family that it was time to leave Pekur's kin to rejoice alone. Yambunapan and his male agnates acquiesced, taking with them their bride-price. Significantly, they left behind Bibi's mother, maternal aunts, and a few of Yambunapan's sisters who, knowing

Bibi still to be their child, blended into the throng of dancing and singing women.

The idiom of male and female relationships

The hostility expressed by the agnates of Yambunapan and those of Pekur in their oratory was neither intended nor understood as an attempt of one to establish domination over the other. Since all Chambri recognize that they owe their lives to those who have provided their women, a wife-giving group is assumed to have an unshakable superiority over any of its wife-taking groups. Although wife-givers and wife-takers may use their rhetoric to negotiate in some measure the particular level of inequality which should prevail between them, the most general objective of their public speeches is to appear as consummate wife-givers or wife-takers to those unrelated groups with whom competition for actual superiority or control does exist.

The message conveyed through this rhetoric was that, despite their relationship of inequality, each clan could demand its rights because it was strong. This assertion of strength was particularly important for members of Pekur's clan to convey because they had been patronized in the past by several different clans. Yambunapan's clan, in contrast, was much better established. Yambunapan's older brother, Kapiwan, described in the anthropological literature for his violence and wealth (see Mead, 1935), was still recognized throughout the Middle Sepik as a powerful sorcerer. Both brothers were descended from the first *Luluai* of Kilimbit Village.[7] Understandably, this clan wished to maintain its reputation for power, particularly in this affinal encounter with those culturally defined as beholden to it.

Theo Pekur's younger brother, therefore, probably intended to appear audacious by asserting to such exceptionally powerful affines that he and his clan had abandoned all rights to Bibi by accepting a large bride-price. His statement was an effective counter to that of Bibi's clan brother, who had proclaimed his clan's superiority over Pekur's by implying – while denying – that Bibi might betray her husband. She might, he was suggesting, even prefer clan endogamy to her marriage with a member of Pekur's group. Since members of a large and affluent clan do occasionally marry one another (primarily because no other group can afford to maintain adequate affinal exchanges with them), Bibi's clan brother was flaunting the strength of his group while challenging the capacity of Pekur and his clan to act as satisfactory wife-takers.

In this confrontation, neither clan wished to deprive the other of economic viability and prestige. Affines lose both status and valuable resources if their wife-takers fail to maintain an appropriate level of affinal recompense. Indeed, if Pekur began to neglect his wife-givers, then they would be thought foolish for having agreed to a marriage into his clan. Nor do wife-takers benefit if their wife-givers lose power since that in turn will reduce their own significance. They would not have the opportunity to establish their prestige by maintaining a high level of affinal payment, nor would they continue to derive importance from raising a large bride-price for a woman whose clan became insignificant.

Thus, Theo Pekur's younger brother and Bibi's clan brother, however much they wished to test each other's mettle, were primarily directing their bravado elsewhere, to those unrelated groups whose failure could, in fact, mean their success. It is these groups which provide the context for the formation of relationships between patrons and clients and for the accumulation and loss of power.

However, as we have already seen, a man achieves worth not only as a member of a clan sufficiently impressive to acquire clients, but as the leader of such a clan. Through the marriage of his son, Pekur hoped to demonstrate that the clan he led was of sufficient importance that he had acquired as much power as those who had caused him. This is what Pekur meant to suggest the day after his son's marriage when he shouted to those assembled at another wedding celebration: "I have won. My grandmother's bride-price was \$K75.00. My mother's bride-price was \$K84.00. I have won." By acquiring Bibi for well over what the predecessors of his clan had spent upon these women, he asserted that he had superseded them and thereby established his own worth.[8]

Pekur's immediate frame of reference for validating himself was, thus, his own agnatic group. However, regardless of the degree by which Pekur had superseded the capabilities of his agnatic ascendants, his success would not be generally recognized unless his clan was at the same time regarded as relatively powerful. Significantly, while claiming to have bested those who acquired his grandmother and mother, Pekur did not mention that he had also paid more for Bibi than his senior agnates had paid for his own wife. Pekur's wife had in fact been acquired for a very low bride-price at a time when the clan had been extremely poor – indeed, had been a

Photograph 7. The new bride calmly prepares sago pancakes for the other women

client. To indicate what had been paid for her relative to Bibi would have been humiliating rather than aggrandizing because it would have suggested that those Pekur has superseded were themselves undistinguished.

Pekur's effort to avoid reference to the amount paid for his wife was of little avail. "Yes, Pekur", said the man coordinating the second wedding ceremony, "you have pulled a lot of money. But I, without the help of my brothers, paid more for my *second* wife than you, with the help of your kin, paid for Bibi." Pekur, obviously deflated by this complex comparison which reminded the assembled guests of his wife's low cost, while it reduced his accomplishment in so generously compensating Yambunapan could only reply: "Yes, we both pulled a lot of money. We are both big men."

It is in this way, through the competition between and within clans that each man attempts to capture and display more than his share of the limited power available. That this strategy of validation is contrary to the strategy pursued by women is nowhere better seen than in the sago-frying ceremony through which the women of the clan – the wives, sisters and mothers – welcome a new bride. On the

Photograph 8.   A woman, behaving as a child, stuffs raw sago down her throat

day when Pekur was proclaiming his own worth to his competitors from other clans, the women of his and various other groups were again using the occasion of the marriage to demonstrate relations of solidarity rather than of competitive opposition.

At this ceremony the bride and perhaps one or two other young women who had recently married into the clan calmly prepared sago pancakes for all women, regardless of clan, who wished to "behave like children." And, to the amusement of both male and female bystanders, behave like children they did: crying that their "mother" loved another more than them; helping cook the food by putting out the fire; hitting one another with coconut-frond brooms while screeching that this or that one had already eaten her share; plopping themselves down into their "mother's" lap and reaching for her breast to take a drink; singing children's songs; throwing handfuls of raw sago at one another; and stuffing raw sago down their own and others' throats.

In this ceremony women ignore the distinctions of age and kinship just as they do when they crawl between one another's legs, calling those "mother" from whom they were "given birth." By becoming their child's child, daughter-in-law's daughter, niece's newborn or even sister's child, women of various clans seek to ignore those constraints which impede them from becoming their own mothers.

Marriage, thus, is a context which provides both men and women with their own kind of opportunity to exhibit equality through replicating their predecessors. Although the inclination of men is to sharpen agnatic distinctions, and that of the women to dull them, they nonetheless frequently view the activities of the other with bemused tolerance and good will as entirely appropriate.

Chapter 8

The monetization of social relationships

Throughout this book we have argued that the strategies followed by Chambri to achieve value are based on fundamental cultural premises. Thus we have seen that Chambri men and women, who define themselves positionally as members of social networks and who regard the universe as subject to entropic processes, strive to acquire worth by attempting to replicate those who have caused their being.[1] But what of the future?

In this chapter we consider what effect the increasingly pervasive use of money has had and may continue to have on affinal relationships. When women were given as wives in exchange for shell valuables, they were not regarded as purchased objects worth a certain number of shells, but rather as embodiments of affinal relationships of enduring inequality. Now that the women are acquired with the same medium of exchange as are a vast array of commodities – such as outboard motors which can be owned outright – the possibility arises that women may acquire some of the attributes of commodities and affinal relations may become largely commercial.[2]

Indeed, we will consider several recent cases in which affines have speculated as to whether exceptionally high bride-prices might be sufficient to retire the affinal debt. Affines may also have begun to regard the help they give their sisters' sons as an investment rather than as an expression of matrilateral nurture. To the extent that social relations become substantially monetized in these ways, the concept and experience of ontological debt and, consequently, the way in which personal worth is defined and established are likely to undergo substantial change.[3]

Clemence Akaman comes home

Clemence Akaman is now one of the few junior Chambri men who has enough money to contribute generously to affinal exchanges.[4] He is a teacher at a primary school located just outside of Wewak, as is his wife, a Chambri woman whom he describes as "my colleague from Kilimbit Village." The school provides a low-rent house for the couple, and their remaining expenses are easily met by their two salaries.[5] During the Christmas holidays, 1983, Clemence and his wife returned to Chambri Island. Clemence's wife had borne a child during the previous year, and they wished to introduce their infant daughter to her relatives back home. But of more importance, Clemence, arriving resplendent in the newest and smartest European clothes, carrying a clip-board and a huge radio-cassette player, had been asked to "go first" in raising the bride-price for his classificatory brother.

The Chambri recognize the social role of "going first" on a bride-price or other affinal payment. The person holding this position must give the most or, at least, a significant amount of money and he must have the power to "pull" money from others. It is a substantial responsibility and the one that Pekur assumed in accumulating the bride-price described in the last chapter.

Clemence contributed $K120.00 from his own savings, and was eventually able to convince 33 other people to donate $K590.00, in amounts ranging from $K2.00 to $K30.00, for a total bride-price of $K710.00. He was pleased with this performance because, though still a young man (only 24 years old), he had raised more than was necessary to satisfy the prospective wife-givers who, as members of an undistinguished clan, had expected only $K500.00. Clemence's agnates had badly needed his help and he, in his turn, had been delighted to show off his powers at home. He was, in fact, the only one of his clan capable of contributing a large sum of money.

Although several of Clemence's agnates did acquire some money from time to time through the sale of artifacts, fish and livestock, none had a regular income. Nor were any of them soon likely to find a job since most businesses in places such as Wewak kept signs permanently posted in their windows announcing in Neo-Melanesian, "Sorry, we have no work." Clemence owed his own financial success, he believed, to his education. Indeed, another important reason that he and his wife returned home was to repay those who had contributed to his school fees and other educational expenses.

Photograph 9. The approach to Chambri Island blocked by *Salvinia molesta*

In the same evening that Clemence and his agnates collected the bride-price, they also raised $K129.00 in amounts ranging from $K2.00 to $K20.00, to repay five affines who had previously helped him pay fees and other school expenses. (Agnates had assisted as well but were not – and never are – directly repaid.) These contributors had correctly assumed that they would be generously recompensed once Clemence graduated and found work, in the same way that they would have been recompensed by a boy's agnates for providing him with food during initiation. Education has, indeed, come to be regarded as comparable to initiation.

Although education is not a substitute for initiation, it is perceived to be as necessary as initiation for the transformation of a child into an active and competent exchanger.[6] Without education, many of our Chambri informants lamented, it is impossible to find work, and without work there is little money. To illustrate: Pekur, who serves on the Catholic Mission school board, wanted us to write a letter for him to the Minister of Education protesting what he believed to be the inordinately high proportion of Standard Six students excluded from entering high school. He knew that without at least some secondary education, young men and women could not find jobs. Pointing to those now called "Standard Six dropouts," he asked us: "Why have we educated these children at all, if we do not allow them to go to high school and then find work? They just play string-band music all day long. They earn no money and are no good to any one."

Only in the last few years have such numbers of young men been regarded as failures. Between the early 1960s and the late 1970s, when labor migration to plantations ceased, Chambri men were readily able to acquire cash through the production and sale of tourist artifacts. Since that time, Sepik lakes and waterways have become choked by an introduced South American fern, *Salvinia molesta*. Few tourists or artifact buyers now trouble to make what has become a difficult trip to Chambri; moreover, transportation costs have now become so high that few Chambri can afford to travel back and forth between Chambri and towns such as Wewak where tourists can still – in ever diminishing numbers – be found.[7] Nor can they easily stay on in Wewak in order to produce their artifacts there: the extremely adverse effect of *Salvinia* on fishing and local trade has made it difficult for Chambri in Wewak to be supported through regular gifts of smoked fish and sago from home.

Thus, while young men just 10 years before were able to act as effective wage earners without much education and, frequently, without even leaving Chambri, the present school dropouts are thought of as largely useless. Stuck in the village because they are ill-trained to find employment in town, the Standard Six dropouts are regarded by their senior agnates such as Pekur as unable to make any significant financial contribution.

Pekur was no doubt quite aware that his own recent political activities had rested on the capacity of his own relatively well educated son, Theo, to find work and in Theo's willingness to allow his father to convert his wages into social networks within the village. Certainly clan viability – indeed, its success – has become dependent upon the contributions of wage earners. Chambri affines and agnates are, therefore, quite correct in viewing education – and the jobs it leads to – as crucial to a young man's coming of age, if the young man is to contribute significantly to the politics of affinal exchange.

However, the fact that affines both give money in payment for the school expenses of their sisters' sons and receive money in compensation may signal an important change in the relations between affines: the debts engendered in the context of education, thus, may well come to have a clearly different meaning from those expressed in initiation.

At the time of a boy's seclusion during his initiation, the mother's brother, in particular, gives him food which represents the matrilateral life-giving nurture. The boy's father then gives the mother's brother a counter gift, as mentioned, which acknowledges the continuing indebtedness of wife-takers to wife-givers. As long as the gifts of wife-takers, whether in the present form of money or the earlier form of valuables, remain qualitatively distinct from those of the wife-givers, affinal exchanges reiterate the basis of affinal inequality: debts to wife-givers can never be fully repaid because women are forever different from that which is received for them. The assumption that the contributions of wife-givers and wife-takers are incommensurable is less likely to remain unchallenged now that both are expressing their respective nurture and obligation through a common medium. The threat to these relationships becomes particularly great when the common medium of exchange between affines is money.

Since money can be used for purchases as different from one another as food, gasoline, outboard motors, transistor radios, cinema tickets, and beer, then any expenditure of money is likely to involve a choice among alternatives. And since money can be spent in so many ways, it cannot easily represent any alternative in particular. In this respect it differs significantly from the traditional items of affinal exchange. The food a mother's brother gives at initiation is readily understood to represent nurture because food is used primarily to nourish. In contrast, the money a mother's brother gives to his sister's son for his education is likely to dilute the message of nurture insofar as money can be used in so many non-nurturing ways. Consequently, a mother's brother's support may no longer represent that which only wife-givers can provide.

To the extent that wife-givers are no longer defining their contribution as that which only wife-givers can make, they are undermining the relationship of enduring debt that is the basis for the special treatment they receive from wife-takers. Wife-takers' contribution of money could be regarded as any commercial transaction, subject to the same appraisals. For instance, wife-givers might regard the money they spend on the education of a sister's son as they would a business investment. Wife-takers in their turn might evaluate these contributions in terms of the economic cost of repayment. Moreover, if affinal exchanges become comparable to other commercial transactions, there is the possibility that payment of cash may confer disposal rights. In this latter eventuality, an affinal relationship would terminate on the conclusion of the business deal.

Certainly there have been recent events which suggest that the relationship between wife-givers and wife-takers is changing. Wife-givers now do in fact complain, at least to third parties, if they do not receive sufficient cash repayment for the money they have spent on their sisters' sons. Wife-takers, for their part, are beginning to entertain the idea that wife-givers can be fully paid off for their contributions. This, in turn, suggests that if affinal inequality can be overcome through the use of money, then affinal relations may become directly competitive, or, on the other hand, entirely dissolved.

The marriage Clemence Akaman had come home to effect was clearly shaped by these trends. As soon as the members of his clan raised the bride-price, they decided to proceed immediately with the money to the bride's house and fetch her forthwith. After all, the $K710.00 was substantially more than her kin had expected for her. Some of the bystanders objected, however, including Pekur, who was acting in this context as a member of the wife-giving family. What shocked him, he told everyone present, was that the wife-takers would think that their bride-price entitled them to acquire the girl whenever they chose. Her agnates, he reminded everyone, were not expecting the bride-price until the following day and would not be prepared to send the necessary household possessions with their daughter as part of her patrimony until that time.

None of the wife-takers heeded these objections and marched immediately to the house of the bride's father. There, as the father sat with his head in his hands humiliated (his sister told us) by the behavior of his affines, they took his daughter from him. She was not even given time to dress in the finery she had prepared for the occasion. Escorted alone, without a companion "sister," the bride wept violently throughout the walk back to her husband's father's house. Because she and her agnates had been caught at such a disadvantage, she was unable to compose herself for her introduction into her husband's group.

Clemence admitted to us that something – he was not quite sure what – had gone awry. It seemed to us, as we observed this marriage, that these wife-takers, by pulling the bride from her father at their convenience and by preventing him from preparing the traditional counter-display, were offering a challenge to the established nature of the affinal relationship. Clemence's clan was acting as if the bride-price they had paid was at least equal in worth to that of the bride and hence cancelled their debt to her agnates. They were suggesting that if the bride-price was high enough, then the acquisition of a wife need not result in a relationship of fundamental enduring indebtedness.

There were other suggestions in the round of some six marriages transacted this Christmas season that the way in which women were evaluated and, hence, the nature of affinal debt and relationship, might have changed. In one of the speeches we described at the post-nuptial celebration held for Theo Pekur and Bibi Yambun, Theo Pekur's younger brother had told Bibi's agnates that the money they had been paid was sufficient to compensate them for any future damage inflicted upon their daughter. As an assertion of clan strength this speech was, as we have stated, typical for this occasion; however, the specific contention expressed was not.

He was stating in his rhetoric that the bride-price he and his agnates had paid for Bibi should provide them with complete rights of ownership. This implied that Bibi might be regarded as an investment similar to that in any commodity, such as an outboard motor or a pickup truck. Thus, if the acquisition of a bride comes to be generally viewed primarily as a monetary transaction, no social relationship will be necessarily established between wife-givers and wife-takers. To the extent that the education of a sister's son or the acquisition of a bride are regarded as investments, there need be no assumption that an enduring social relationship exists which is embodied in the persons of the son/nephew or the daughter/wife.

On remaining Chambri

While looking through some Chambri memorabilia, Deborah recently came upon a drawing made in 1974 by seven-year-old Lucy Sai, which anticipates the social alterations that Clemence Akaman, Theo Pekur's younger brother and others were sensing. Perhaps because her mission education had somewhat prepared her for Western social relationships, Lucy, in 1974, became a particularly good friend of Deborah's four-year-old daughter, Alexis, and

Photograph 10.   Four-year-old Alexis with Chambri friends

Figure 5.   Suburban Chambri

Photograph 11. The only remaining full-sized men's house

together they engaged in the "mommy" and "house" fantasies which preoccupied many little Western girls at that time. Alexis had brought with her several of the props necessary to engage in these fantasies and her grandparents sent additional picture books, dolls and their accessories (including a "Barbie" doll, described by Lucy in Chambri as the "skinny" baby).

Lucy's drawing, Figure 5, reflects the games in which she and Alexis created and recreated social arrangements for these dolls as if the two girls were living in a suburb of any American city rather than in the lowlands of the East Sepik Province. In her drawing Lucy depicts her Chambri village as consisting entirely of small, identically constructed houses, each with a single coconut palm to the side and a happy housewife in the doorway. Although Lucy could not have known it when she drew this picture, all three Chambri villages have come in fact to resemble her childhood image of them. The individualizing influences she encountered in her schooling and in her friendship with Alexis are part of and consistent with the influences that virtually all Chambri have been experiencing.

The large women's houses of Lucy's childhood, designed to

Photograph 12.   A modern and abbreviated men's house

shelter an extended family, have all but disappeared as a result of changes in household size and composition.[8] The large houses functioned as maps of family solidarity and affinal interdependence. To illustrate: One of the remaining large Indingai houses has a central post carved with totemic emblems and draped with clan ceremonial gear and called Marliriman after an apical ancestor of the house-owning family. On either side of this central post, and supporting the thatched roof, are five additional carved posts, each called by an ancestral name of the particular agnate whose domestic area surrounds the post. Each of a man's wives, in turn, has placed her cooking hearth in his area of the house and fastened there the totemically significant hook she was given by her agnates on which to hang the basket containing her patrimony of shells. Such a house was, in reality, a replication of the social relationships of the clan.

These large clan houses have become anachronistic. The increasing use of money has not only made it less important but more difficult for clansmen to live together. In other words, a clan's viability is less dependent upon the number and solidarity of its members than on the remittances of its wage-earners. Moreover, those who do earn money wish to assert disposal rights over that

Photograph 13.   Yorondu, Atlas-like, under the eaves

which they have purchased, such as radios, tape-recorders and watches, and are reluctant for these possessions to circulate freely within the clan. Clan members prefer, we were explicitly told, to have separate domestic dwellings to keep these privately purchased

goods safe from agnatic claims. Even those few remaining poly-
gynists are likely to provide separate houses for their wives in order
to establish a separate domestic economy for each wife.[9]

For similar reasons, the large and elaborate men's houses also are
becoming replaced by houses comparable in construction and size
to the new single family house. Of the 15 men's houses still
recognized as belonging within the three Chambri villages, the only
full-sized one standing in 1984 was in Wombun Village. It was built
about 1976 by men from all three villages to attract tourists to
Chambri and to house the artifacts offered them for sale. Two other
large men's houses standing until recently – one in Indingai and the
other in Kilimbit – collapsed in 1982. The houses which would
replace each were under construction when we arrived the following
year. These were small and lacked virtually all of the significant
traditional features such as the elaborately carved posts to mark the
particular location of clan identity and power within the encompass-
ing structure.

One morning while we watched Yorondu working alone on
Indingai's new men's house, 10 Standard Six dropouts were playing
their guitars and ukuleles in a nearby group. Yorondu told us with
anger and resignation that it was now impossible to build a men's
house in the correct fashion – to build one which contained the
symbolic themes of cosmological unity and social demarcation –
because there were too few men from the necessary social groups
willing to take on the task. With clan viability now so greatly
dependent on the infrequent visits and remittances of largely urban
wage earners, the large men's houses, like the large dwelling houses,
have become anachronistic.

Moreover, few men were at this time willing to contribute to the
construction of even this abbreviated men's house. Most of the older
men were preoccupied with the spate of Christmas weddings, and
the school dropouts were proclaiming their disinterest. Recognizing
that they could make no contribution to the politics of affinal
exchange which still preoccupied their elders, these young men were
indicating their identification with the world of popular music and
Western goods.[10] As we left Yorondu to his solitary labors, he
asked us to take a picture of him. He stood, Atlas-like, under the
eaves, apparently to show that he, at least, was supporting his
culture.

Indeed, Yorondu not only knows how to construct a men's house,
but how to summon a clan to a men's house with its own slit-gong

rhythm. He knows how to initiate within a men's house, and how to ensorcell those who abandon their men's house and their totemic responsibilities. He knows the esoteric names of hundreds of totemically significant rocks in the three Chambri villages, and as he walks through his landscape of signification, he consorts with ancestors. Yet, Yorondu, because he has no means of earning money, has become incapable of contributing to the affinal exchanges that would mark him as a man of power. Indeed, he can contribute little to exchanges of any kind. On one evening, for instance, he crept into our house after consuming eight bottles of beer provided by Yarapat, Pekur and others who were drinking rounds. He had been forced to flee before his turn to buy had come and was ashamed because he was thereby revealed as having no money.[11]

He is, thus, in many ways the opposite of Clemence Akaman, who also finds it difficult to achieve recognition as a man of power. Clemence has been too long away at school and work to have learned much about totemic secrets; certainly he did not have the knowledge of tradition necessary to build a ceremonial house or participate in a men's house debate. Indeed, he could answer few of the questions we asked him about his own culture more completely than by saying, "It's our custom." Nor did he have much understanding even of the practices of the recent Chambri past. Although interested in Deborah's book, *Sepik River Societies*, he did not realize, for instance, that even within his own lifetime, women had bartered their fish for sago from the Sepik Hills or that fish and sago were conceived of as "marrying" one another at these barter markets. Yet, it is undeniably true that Clemence is a very useful Chambri: he earns a good income and is willing to contribute money to the objectives of his senior agnates. But, it is also true that to be a useful Chambri nowadays often means, in terms of cultural knowledge, to be hardly a Chambri at all.

Growing up in New Guinea

Lucy Sai came of age in this world where individuals are increasingly less likely to become completely competent Chambri. She did so, moreover, not at Chambri, but at Kreer Camp, a settlement on the outskirts of Wewak. Over the past 15 years, Chambri migrants have arranged their houses there in three zones, one for each of the three Chambri home villages. Marriages and even initiations are occasionally celebrated at Kreer and men still contend with each other in improvised men's houses. But, Kreer Camp is also a place where rent is paid to others who own the land on which the houses are built and where subsistence is almost entirely dependent on money.

Akapina Sai, Lucy's mother, had moved to Kreer in 1978. After one of her trips to Wewak to sell fish, Akapina decided that she, Lucy, and her other young children would remain permanently in town. No one contested her decision since her husband was dead and his agnates had decided not to keep her as a wife to their clan since they could not afford to continue their affinal obligations to her kin.[12] By 1980, Akapina had taken up residence with Lucas, a Chambri from Indingai Village who had been living in Wewak for over 12 years.

Lucas had become quite prosperous and influential in Wewak through the sale of beer. Although he paid no formal bride-price for Akapina, he did shelter and feed the agnates of Akapina and of her dead husband when they came to town.[13] Neither set of agnates protested this arrangement, nor has Lucas found it economically burdensome. He was, and still is, able to provide generously for these guests and for Akapina and her children. Nor did he object to the addition of another dependent to his household when 15-year-old Lucy bore Bobby.

Lucas did, however, insist on defining the conditions under which he would allow Lucy to marry Bobby's father, a young man who had come to Wewak from the Murik Lakes. Although Akapina's dead husband's agnates would expect a share in any bride-price Lucy might fetch, they were willing to leave to Lucas any negotiations taking place in Wewak. Lucas demanded $K3,000 in bride-price for Lucy which was a sum so great as immediately to drive Bobby's father away.

Lucas justified to us such an extraordinarily high bride-price by explaining that if Lucy were to marry a non-Chambri, her husband would be unlikely to maintain his affinal obligations. The bride-price under these conditions must, therefore, be sufficiently high to cover the full sequence of affinal payments and to compensate for the loss of future social relationships. If Lucas were to become a wife-giver to a Murik Lake clan, he would be deprived both of Lucy's son as a political ally and of wife-takers who continued to acknowledge that they owed him for the fact of their being. However, although Lucas clearly recognized that social relationships were to be valued for their own sake, he was nonetheless able to put a price on them. Like Theo Pekur's younger brother, he could envision a bride-price high enough to convey disposal rights.

There is yet another threat to affinal relationships. Rather than choose to invest in a bride-price high enough to convey disposal rights, Chambri can also simply divert money away from social networks. Chambri like Clemence do in fact speculate about spending their money in ways that do not advance Chambri clan interests. Moreover, such alternatives are likely to become increasingly attractive, particularly for just those who are able to make strong financial contributions to affinal exchanges. Relatively well-educated Chambri have spent so much of their lives away at school and work that they frequently find much about the nature of affinal exchange and the totemic basis of Chambri clan power obscure and quite peripheral to their normal lives. Yet it is for just these political concerns that they are urged to contribute their earnings. At the same time that they may come to question the strength of their commitments to the preoccupations of their senior agnates, they are also experiencing incorporation into urban life with its patterns of friendship, hospitality and consumption. Indeed, already, a number of Clemence's contemporaries rarely return home from the towns in which they work because they are reluctant to spend their money on affinal exchanges.

All Chambri, whether living at home or in a place like Wewak, must now confront, therefore, the fact that money is a very imprecise substitute for other valuables. Unlike valuables such as shell money, money can be used to define the parameters of relationships in such a way that wife-takers may establish a competitive relationship with their wife-givers or they may divest themselves of their relationships entirely. Money can also be diverted from social relationships through the purchase of items for private consumption. Money can allow Chambri to lead viable lives quite apart from other Chambri, certainly far from Chambri Island.

To the extent that Chambri do withdraw from their social networks and do mediate more of their relationships with others through money, then identity may become more vested in attributes which are regarded as inhering in relatively isolated individuals while, at the same time, social relations in general may become less personal. (See Watt, 1959; Lukes, 1973; Dumont, 1977; MacFarlane, 1978 for discussions of the development of individualism in the West.) If money does enable Chambri to continue to alter, avoid and attenuate their affinal as well as other relationships, and does lead to a shift from positional to a private, subjectivist, definition of person, there would as well be a shift in the criteria and strategies for establishing worth.[14] Regardless of whatever the specific consequences the pervasive use of money may prove to have, the possible changes in Chambri sociocultural experience could be profound.

However, such profound changes are not inevitable. (See, for example, Burridge, 1969.) As members of the world economy in an era of general economic depression, it is not clear what the flow of money to the Chambri will be in the future. Indeed, many Chambri in Wewak and other towns may not be able to remain away from a subsistence economy much longer. They may have to retreat back home to live in a region where they will be even more so than they now are "out of the mainstream of development" (Philpott, 1971: 37).[15]

Nor is it clear what choices the Chambri themselves will make about the form and nature of their social relationships. It is significant that although the possibility has been raised that brides can be purchased outright, none – neither Pekur's new daughter-in-law nor Lucy – has in fact been alienated from her kin. Wife-givers may in the future continue simply to place such a high value on the continuation of social relationships through their daughters and daughters' children that no one will be able to afford the price of the commodities – the wives – offered. Or, Chambri may reaffirm the view that no medium can repay the debt of life.[16]

But what of Lucy and the women of her generation? When we last visited her in Kreer Camp, she was with several friends whose prospects encompass the possibilities now available to Chambri women. One was Tiameri who, at the age of 16, had just failed her entrance examination to high school. Her parents had allowed her to accompany her somewhat older maternal cousin to Wewak for a brief excursion so that she could forget her disappointment. Since her education was concluded, there was no reason why her marriage should be further delayed.

Another girl was talking about eloping with a Iatmul whom she had met in Wewak and fancied. In recent years, a number of Chambri women, attracted by the same alternatives as Clemence and his contemporaries, have sought the affluent life by going off with the young men whom they met in town.[17] Although rarely concerned about the sociopolitical consequences of their alliances to non-Chambri, they often do regret their decisions, especially if they can no longer live in Wewak and have to retreat to unfamiliar communities. There, homesick and without brothers to support them and act as *waus* to their sons, they try to persuade their husbands to live matrilocally. One such young woman married to a school teacher was continually agitating for him to be assigned to Chambri. Lucy's decision not to flout Lucas' wishes by leaving Wewak with Bobby's father was probably based on a recognition that she, like other young Chambri women, might well be unhappy away from her family. Certainly Tiameri did not seem inclined to forsake her Chambri ties.

Without secondary education, neither she nor Lucy anticipated any substantial difference between their lives and that, for instance, of Bibi Yambun. Even if they remained permanently in town, with their Chambri husbands, as had Lucy's own mother, they expected to live with agnates and affines whom they would repay for their support and nurture through their bearing of children. Indeed, the life of Clemence Akaman's wife who has had tertiary education still follows much this same pattern.

The only Chambri woman we knew who had significantly redefined her objectives was, in fact, the cousin who had brought Tiameri into Wewak. Bridgit was returning from her Christmas holidays on Chambri Island to her teaching job at the Marienberg Catholic School. The daughter of a Chambri leader of national importance, she had political judgment so astute that her father was prompted to tell us: "If Bridgit were only a man she would succeed me in politics. She is the strongest of all my kin and has the most understanding." She, despite her father's misgivings, did plan to run for public office and sought to offset what she knew to be the liability of her sex, by remaining unmarried. And, to remain unmarried, she believed, she would have to become a nun. She was the only Chambri we knew to criticize publicly anyone for holding what the Church regarded as superstitions. Her ontological debts were evidently to Christ and were to be repaid through a religiously informed social activism.[18]

In contrast to Bridgit, Lucy has not challenged the course of her Chambri life even though the individualizing influences which had led her as a child to draw Chambri as a suburb have continued to affect her. Although, as we have said, it would now be possible for Chambri to deny the social obligations and reformulate the objectives that have defined Chambri identity, Lucy, Clemence, Theo Pekur's younger brother, and Lucas have not chosen to do so.

Photograph 14.   Alexis, Lucy and Bobby

Indeed, Lucy in the 10 years since Alexis first knew her had remained so much a member of her culture that Alexis, at 14, found her old friend difficult to understand. While reading *Jane Eyre* and *Wuthering Heights* on her revisit to New Guinea in 1983, Alexis had become convinced that the experience of others could help her understand her own particular feelings.[19] Lucy, remembered fondly as an intimate, had just suffered, from Alexis' perspective, a reversal in romance, assuming she had loved Bobby's father. That Lucy was neither distraught nor even distressed at the loss of her Heathcliffe was incomprehensible. Nor was it clear to Alexis how Lucy's adolescent sexual experience – and the birth of her child – could have occurred with so little personal or social upheaval. Alexis discovered that Lucy was happy at Kreer Camp: she had enough money to feed herself and her son; she had friends and kin with whom to leave him on occasion; and although she expected to marry she was not concerned that she be in love with her husband. Lucy was, thus, in Kreer Camp still very much a Chambri.

Both girls were finding as they came of age that becoming friends as children a decade before had been easier than remaining so.

Conclusion
The significance of cultural alternatives

At the beginning of this book we examined the political implications of a *Time* magazine article and a cartoon it contained. The article charged Margaret Mead with exaggerating the extent of cultural differences, while the cartoon suggested that the only thing of importance one can learn from non-Western peoples is that it is boring to be one of them.

We argued that the cartoon in particular conveyed a reactionary perspective by suggesting that there are no real cultural alternatives. Our present data, about male and female relationships in a society which operates with a set of non-Western cultural premises, can, we think, support a contrasting view.

In this concluding chapter, we must reflect upon ourselves and ask about the intellectual and political significance of what we have accomplished. We present in this regard another cartoon, drawn by Carolyn Hillyer for the *Women's Studies International Forum*, a journal dedicated to publishing multidisciplinary articles concerning women's lives (1983: 329).

As can be seen, this cartoon depicts two women, writing and doing research between the anthropology and sociology sections of a library, while feminists protest an unspecified issue outside the building in the rain. One of the two scholars expresses guilt, recognizing that because it is always dry in libraries her comfort is assured while others protest on her behalf. To her guilt we would add our own, and attempt to reciprocate the efforts of those in the rain by speaking as anthropologists to the feminist issues of significance to social activists. We are concerned, therefore, to use our understanding of the Chambri to contribute to the process of generating and appraising proposals for effecting gender equality in our own lives.[1]

By committing ourselves to such an effort we are adopting Mead's

129

Cartoon 2.

own perspective that other lives in other places have significance for us by demonstrating the range of human possibilities. We do, however, differ from her about the nature of meaning of the lives of Chambri men and women and, therefore, also differ from her in our view of what the particular relationship is between these lives and our own.

Mead was wrong, we have said, in arguing that the Chambri reversed the sex roles which existed in our own society. She thought Chambri women dominated over their men primarily because she regarded Chambri women as behaving in the way that men do in our own society. However, according to our analysis, Chambri women do not act like American men, nor, for that matter, like American women; Chambri men, moreover, do not act like either.

Indeed, the Chambri are sufficiently unlike Mead's Westernized portrait that it is difficult to regard them as providing any *direct* model for us at all. Alexis, for instance, would not wish to become a Lucy defining herself in positional terms, however satisfied Lucy may be with her own life, since this would mean that Alexis would have to give up that which is most important to her. Nor, correspondingly, would a Chambri woman wish to have a private and subjective self. Such a self – defined in terms of a set of relatively unique dispositions, capacities and perspectives – would make her profoundly isolated and disoriented in Chambri culture. The concept of person by which individuals shape their sense of self, the definition of individual worth and the strategies of men and women are, we have concluded, substantially different for the Chambri than for ourselves and form very different sorts of individuals in each case.[2]

(We consider these terms – positional and subjective – to convey accurately the contrast between Chambri and American concepts of person. We do not, however, assume that the concepts of person which prevail in other cultures should necessarily be so categorized. Moreover, it should be noted that even when persons are defined primarily in terms of their social position, the requirements and the arrangement of these positions – and, thus, the nature and relationship of persons – will vary from society to society. Hence, for example, the differences between Chambri and Balinese societies mean that persons in each case, although defined positionally are, nonetheless, very different from each other [see Geertz, 1966].

On subjectivity and work

If Chambri lives cannot be direct models for our own, we may be able to understand the system of sociocultural assumptions and constraints which are now shaping our own lives if we compare our system with theirs. We may be able to clarify the interests of women living in contemporary America – perhaps in the contemporary West as a whole – by understanding what the interests are of women living in sociocultural contexts different from our own. When Western feminists press for social change, the kind of society they may envision which would enable people to derive more satisfaction from their lives may make more sense to us if we understand why it would make less sense to the Chambri.

The principal contrasts between Chambri interests and our own stem not only from the differences between positional and subjective definitions of person, but also from the relative value of continuity and discontinuity.[3] Whereas Chambri acquire validity by replicating the positions, and thus the identities, of those who caused them, we acquire validity through developing unique subjectivities that let us diverge from the identities of those who caused us. Our Western view that persons are best defined through their novel subjectivities results in strategies which, at present, focus on the achievement of socially valued forms of individuality.[4]

Such an individuality is thought to result from a process of controlling and tempering the subjectivity of a child through the introduction of what are regarded as objective constraints, the constraints which are thought to characterize the world at large. Children must develop their sense of themselves as distinctive and competent individuals without remaining entirely self-absorbed. To the extent that this development is successful, a person will be regarded as mature, as having achieved the kind of individuality that marks him or her as an adult.[5] If a person fails in this development, s/he will be regarded as having an improperly shaped subjectivity – as dependent, irrational, unreasonable, and impulsive in ways that mark him or her still as a child.[6]

For subjectivity to receive validation, that is, for one to be regarded as a person of worth, as a mature adult, comparisons must be made with other subjectivities. Only through comparison can a person measure the degree to which s/he is unique as well as competent and social – the degree, that is, to which s/he has achieved a valued individuality. Moreover, s/he is likely to seek confirmation of his or her own judgment through the judgment of others.[7] Since one's view of oneself is only one's own view – since one may recognize that one's view of one's own subjectivity may be too subjective – one may seek to establish a more objective judgment through receiving the validation of others.

The implications of this need for the objective validation of personal worth pervade American sociocultural life. Indeed, we argue that the differential access to the process of validation is a major determinant of the ways that individuals experience gender relationships: much of the significance of work and consumption in our society derives from their importance as major contexts in which men and women can display, compare and evaluate their subjectivities.

(As a preface to our discussion of the way in which American men and women employ strategies for achieving worth through work and consumption, we wish to indicate that work need not inevitably alienate a worker from his or her product and that individuality need not inevitably be based on competitive consumption.)

The division of labor which characterizes work in our society specifies the relative value and distinctiveness of each worker. The amount of money received for work provides what is regarded as at least a roughly objective measure – given a supply and demand view of economics – of the degree to which a set of occupational skills is defined as special. A quite average auto worker hence can be thought a person of some worth, despite the fact that there may be hundreds of others on his shift – and thousands more in his union. His pay scale and his capacity to affect major portions of the economy through slowdown or strike are interpreted as providing objective verification of the relative value of his skills.[8]

Forms of work are appraised as desirable according to the degree that an occupation can validate personal worth. A "good job," in contrast to a "lousy job," pays well, allows initiative and is interesting: it thus confers what is interpreted as a largely objective judgment of merit for the development and expression of special skills.[9] It is worthy of note that the better a job is by these criteria, the more likely it is to be held by a man than by a woman. Even in repetitive jobs requiring little skill, men are more likely to receive higher wages, and thus more validation, than are women. In addition, women have a more contingent role in the work force than do men since their jobs are defined as not only less important but less permanent.[10]

In Bujra's view:

Even when women enter the labour market they do not shake off their situational disabilities as domestic labourers. As Beechey (1977) has argued, female wage labourers cannot be considered as structurally equivalent to male workers. They can be paid wages that fall beneath the value (the cost of reproduction) of their labour power, since these costs of reproduction are already taken account of in their husbands' wages ... "[T]he role of the domestic labourer, though highly specialized, is a socially dependent one. While vital to capitalism, it appears in a trivialized form as non-work". (1978: 22)[11]

The conclusion Bujra reaches – that women, whether or not they actually hold jobs, are defined in substantial measure through their non-work, their domestic labor – can be supported by other sorts of evidence. When married women work outside the home they still assume primary responsibility for housework. (According to 1982 statistics, nearly 49 per cent of all married women with children under the age of six and just over 63 per cent with children over the age of six do have jobs. Overall, more than 51 per cent of wives work [Tavris and Wade, 1984: 269].) Indeed, "[o]n average, employed

wives spend twenty-six hours a week on housework – their husbands, thirty-six minutes" (Tavris and Wade, 1984: 286). The same
pattern holds true for child care with the average American father
spending only 12 minutes a day with his children (Tavris and Wade,
1984: 287). The evidence, thus, both about the kinds of jobs women
are likely to have and the amount of time they spend on domestic
labor, suggests that the degree to which women can identify
themselves as workers is restricted by the strength of their commitment to the home. Indeed, even those women who have what are
regarded as better jobs are comparably restricted.[12]

The implications of this circumstance for gender relationships, it
seems to us, are these: to the extent that a woman's identity is that of
a non-worker, her worth as a person is likely to be evaluated as less
than that of a man.[13] Because domestic labor is unpaid and
relatively private it does not provide as powerful a validation of
individuality as does work.

Not only is housework unpaid, but it is also regarded as within the
capacity of virtually all women. There is, thus, the double implication that competence per se in this area confers little distinction.
To the extent that women remain categorized in major respects as
non-workers in a culture which values individuality, they – including those women with jobs – are likely to compete with each other to
distinguish themselves as having domestic skills which go beyond
simple competence.[14] Individuality is established through demonstrating superior ability to manage the family budget, to keep
children well behaved, to get everything done, to have special
talents in cooking, etc.[15] These domestic skills, indeed, remain the
subject of much conversation, not only among housewives in the
neighborhood but among women as they work at their jobs.[16]
However, because the locus of domestic activity is the home and the
number of their peers is restricted to friends, neighbors or proximate
co-workers, the available range of comparison is likely to be small
and the degree of consensual – hence, objective – validation is thus
likely to be limited.

Certainly, if a woman actually does spend her days at home, her
activities there are likely to contrast unfavorably to the work her
husband is doing at the same time.[17] Moreover, housework falls
somewhere between work and leisure. Just as it does not provide the
relative prestige of the former, it does not provide the opportunity
for relaxation and self-expression of the latter. Hence, when her
husband returns home from his work, his waiting wife is not as free

as he to express herself through leisure activities. She is not entitled to leisure since she has not actually been working.[18] Leisure is equally elusive, as we have seen, for women returning home after their work who find their domestic obligations awaiting them.[19]

Because this domestic work is unpaid, it is defined as motivated by love. Whereas money is thought to be an objective and universal measure of worth, love is thought to be a subjective and highly particular recognition of worth. Love is regarded as based on responses between unique individuals who know each other so well and who so endorse the worth of the other as to be unconcerned with objective measurements. Indeed, the ideology of love holds that the other is of incomparable – hence, immeasurable – value.[20]

Love, as a form of deep personal commitment, rather than as contractual agreement, means that a woman's domestic services must be offered when they are needed. Thus, when a worker comes home from his job to express his identity in activities of his choice, his wife may have difficulty doing the same – even if she feels she has earned her leisure – since "a woman's work is never done."[21]

Nor by reason of the nature of her tie to her family can she as readily express rebellion in her non-work work as can her husband in his work. When workers feel that their contracts with their employers are unfair – that, for instance, they are not paid or otherwise treated as they think they should be – they will certainly feel justified in changing jobs or going on strike. If they must remain at their jobs, they will often feel entitled to retaliate against their employers through such measures as pilferage, loafing, and sabotage. In this way, workers who cannot afford to leave their jobs may feel that they are negotiating an implicit contract through the reciprocation of devaluation. In contrast, because a wife is supposed to be committed to the members of her family, she should stick with them and, in addition, continue to accept their concerns as her own. Although a coke bottle welded into a body panel may be regarded as acceptably defiant of Ford Motor Company, slime in the shower is interpreted not as a commendable sign of independence but as slovenly disregard of the welfare of one's family.

However, men and women not only define themselves through the nature of their work and non-work, but also through their consumption. How money is spent indicates both earning power and subjectivity: through the display of their tastes, concerns and values, individuals manifest themselves as possessing special dispositions, capacities and perspectives. (See Bourdieu, 1984, for a thorough discussion of this point.) In particular, purchases which are not regarded as necessities in their most basic forms are diagnostic of subjectivity. That an acquisition is defined entirely or in part as non-essential indicates a degree of affluence and thus of social worth; that it is in some measure non-essential means that its purchase was an act of choice which reveals the subjectivity of preference. For instance, in a middle class neighborhood in which everyone has a washing machine, a family can still display its affluence and standards of choice through selecting a model of an expensive brand which is distinctive in its color and in its features.[22]

(Thus, for example, an advertisement appearing recently in our local newspaper encouraged readers to buy an expensive van in the following words: "Success takes many forms. Financial, professional, social and personal achievements create unique transformations in an individual's character and outlook. Since you have established your place in life, you deserve a luxury vehicle that exhibits and exemplifies your conquests – a product reminiscent of your accomplishments" [Daily Hampshire Gazette, October 11, 1985: 28].)

Women would seem to be given a cultural mandate, in part conveyed through advertising, to have a more important role than men in the development and expression of subjectivity through consumption. However, a woman's purchases are to express her subjectivity not only by displaying her taste, concerns, values but, frequently, her love. She is enjoined that "little things mean a lot" to her family. After all, it is she who should select, for example, the clothes that her husband and children wear as well as the curtains, carpet and furniture of their home. Moreover, when she is encouraged to spend a few hours of her busy day with a romantic novel, or to luxuriate in a bubble bath, it is to enjoy and cultivate her feminine subjectivity which will make her appealing to her husband. When she is urged to maintain her self-esteem through dressing attractively and remaining trim through exercise and correct diet, it is again to make her appealing to her husband. And, of course, she is reminded of her responsibility to ensure that her husband's hours at work are not marred by a collar laundered with an ineffective powder nor his hours of leisure spoiled by an abrasive toilet tissue.[23]

All of these displays of subjectivity are predicated on the assumption that her primary role is to express the subjectivity of her love through gratifying and ministering to her family. Very often, in fact, a woman decides to find a job because she wishes to provide a better life for those she loves.[24] Her consumption – and, perhaps even her work – thus becomes a manifestation of her non-work in which she is constrained by the need to serve and thus to please her husband and their children.

Her rewards for this service are relatively uncertain: If she is successful in pleasing her husband and their children, she will receive love in return as well as the satisfaction of having made some difference in their lives. However, not infrequently, husbands fall out of love with their wives, and children rebel. Also, since husbands and children have volition and are subject to a wide variety of influences, it is often unclear what her effects on them have been. Furthermore, to the extent that a husband or child becomes successful, he is likely to take primary credit for what he interprets as his own achievements.

It is, thus, often difficult for a woman to feel validated in the roles of wife and mother. In addition, we contend, even if she does feel that she is of worth, nonetheless, her subjectivity remains in considerable measure contingent on that of her husband.[25] He, after all, is credited with having selected her as his wife and as mother to his children. His choice of her is a meta-choice which subsumes her specific choices. Her "woman's touch," which beautifies herself and the home, ameliorates his life and nurtures his children, is the ultimate consequence of his choice of her.

Although neither men nor women are likely to formulate their relationship in terms of contingency, both frequently recognize that men regard themselves as more important through having established a more socially valued and verified subjectivity – a more substantial and weightier individuality – than women. Because they generally provide greater economic support for their families, men may view their contributions as primary. Because they are regarded as *essentially* workers, men view themselves as more objective, as more mature, because their subjectivities have been more strongly shaped – tempered – by the world at large, the objective world.

Consequently, men often regard women as more subjective: as both childish and sensitive. They see women as somewhat immature: as dependent, irrational, unreasonable, and impulsive. However, because they believe women to be more sensitive, they also regard them as better at interpersonal relationships and as having a more refined aesthetic appreciation. Men can cheerfully acknowledge that women have those practical capacities necessary for domestic or even paid labor, while still denying them full capacity to act in the realm that men define as requiring the most practical judgment and initiative.

Women may accept the claims of their husbands to greater primacy and objectivity or regard these male assertions of import-ance as themselves manifestations of immaturity. Partly because their husbands think that they have through their work earned the right to be attended and deferred to, their wives may regard them as helpless – sometimes endearing – autocrats. Wives may view their husbands as "big babies" who must be placated and managed so that they continue to bring in the money on which family life depends and do not spend it in foolish and impulsive ways. In so managing their husbands – along with their other children, the family budget, the shopping and other tasks – women are able to conclude that theirs is the realm which requires particular practical competence.

However, although men and women may deprecate each other in the same terms, the battle is unequal because to the extent that women are financially dependent non-workers they are in actuality much more likely than men to find their autonomy curtailed and the expression of their subjectivity subsumed. In so far as women are, in fact, contingent, they therefore have greater difficulty in estab-lishing worth in a culture that measures worth in terms of the capacity to demonstrate a distinctive and competent subjectivity: to demonstrate a valued individuality.

For these reasons, anti-feminist efforts to establish personal worth by arguing that the domestic sphere is a domain separate from but equal to that of the men are not likely to result in relationships of equality between men and women. Separate cannot be equal under circumstances of contingency: indeed anti-feminist ideology in its efforts to mark and maintain the boundaries of the domestic sphere seems to be striving for protection from rather than equality with men.[26]

On domination and well-formed lives

We have come to realize more clearly why Deborah sensed a threat to her individuality when Yorondu offered to reveal his sacred clay flute to Frederick rather than to her. Yorondu was defining the fundamental identity of the two ethnographers on the positional basis of their gender; moreover, he was using these categorical criteria to exclude Deborah from something of importance to her identity as a professional anthropologist, simply because she was a woman. Indeed, Deborah was annoyed because she felt that Yorondu was attempting to dominate over her.

Dominance, we have argued in Chapter 3, is that which impedes or prevents an individual from following the strategies necessary to meet the cultural standards which define personal worth. For members of a culture which defines persons in subjectivist terms, acts which are interpreted as depersonalizing are experienced as at least a mild domination: to be *primarily* a member of a category is to lack individuality and thus is, *for us*, to be less than a person of worth. When depersonalization is not just a bureaucratic convenience but is used to preclude access to worth, then it becomes a powerful form of domination.[27]

Yorondu, however, intended no act of domination. Indeed his wife, daughter and visiting kinswomen who continued their conversations outside the house did not object either to being categorized as women or to being displaced for that reason. Because the strategies of Chambri women are completely different from those of Chambri men, they are not inevitably in competition with men. The positional identities of Chambri women are neither inadequate nor contingent. Because they do not compare unfavorably to Chambri men, and are not denied access to cultural standards of worth, Chambri women are, in general, not dominated over by men.[28]

Unlike Chambri women, American women are frequently dominated over – frequently prevented from becoming persons of worth. Defined substantially in terms of their domestic activities, women, whether or not they actually hold jobs, are restricted in their access to the kind of validation which comes through work. Of at least equal importance, however, is the fact that women are not only excluded from this form of validation but are *categorized* in major degree as non-workers: they are non-workers *because* they are women.[29] To be subject to such a categorical definition is inherently depersonalizing in a cultural context which values individuality.[30]

The distinction between work and non-work, therefore, rests on defining women in positional terms as categorically ineligible to engage fully in work. To the extent that women are regarded as non-workers, their role as workers will be defined as marginal. While subscribing to subjectivist values, our society nonetheless imposes positional definitions on some, and in this manner women receive a form of double domination: They have difficulty in defining themselves both as individuals and as individuals of worth through restriction of their access to the validation which comes from work. Thus, women are primarily left to establish individuality in the realm of non-work where, as we have argued, their individuality is likely to remain contingent on and subsumed by that of their husbands.

Thus, domination is inherent in the relations between American men and women to the extent that women are categorically limited in their opportunities to validate their identities through work.[31] In contrast, the Chambri use positional definitions to establish male and female identities and strategies as distinct from each other. Chambri men and women are largely able to allow each other to pursue their separate strategies for acquiring worth, and rarely seek to dominate over each other.

Mead was, thus, quite correct in her perception that Chambri women conducted their lives with more assurance than do American women. When Deborah's mother and her friend found that Margaret Mead's portrayal of the Chambri spoke directly to their own lives it was as much for her portrayal of their sense of unimpeded competence and confidence in performing the activities of Chambri life as in her description of their activities as comparable to those of men in our own society.

Chambri men and women, therefore, teach us that it is not inevitable that male strategies for achieving worth result in the domination of women. And, if the Chambri cannot act as a direct model for us in our efforts to enable American women to achieve worth, they can, as we have argued, help us clarify our objectives.[32] To understand why Alexis would not wish to seek reproductive closure through mother's brother's daughter's marriage is to better understand what the nature of her experience will be if, as a woman, she is categorized as being in major respects a non-worker. To understand the Chambri is to be better able to appraise and pursue those feminist objectives which seek to reorganize our own society so that women may fully develop and express their subjective worth.[33]

The debates on the nature and scope of this reorganization are wide-ranging and cover such issues as the right of a pregnant woman relative to her fetus, the degree of obligation of the state to provide adequate child care for working parents, and the practical and moral justification of reverse discrimination in employment. Debates also consider the need to change the nature and relationship of work and non-work and, in addition, raise the fundamental question of whether American men and women can achieve relations of equality, in this or any other economic system, if they live with each other. Debates also concern whether or not these relations of equality can be achieved without a fundamental shift from, for instance, values of competition to those of cooperation and connectedness. The proposals raised in these debates all concern efforts by women to realize themselves as persons of worth. They can be seen to make sense in terms of our existing cultural premises about subjectivity, individuality and autonomy, although they would differ significantly in their effect on our social organization.

Through comparing the Chambri with ourselves we can, thus, become assured that male dominance is not inevitable and become more clear-sighted concerning the nature of feminist objectives – we can at least know what those outside the library in the rain would find important to hear about their lives and aspirations. We can also better understand the nature of social responsibility in our own culture which includes concern for even those one does not actually know. Our scholar felt guilt at remaining in the library because she recognized that those demonstrating, as well as those they were demonstrating for, were, like herself, all fundamentally equal by reason of their potential worth as subjectivities.[34] She suspected that the relative autonomy of her own subjectivity was based on privilege and that in her silence she was an accomplice in perpetuating social arrangements which curtailed their opportunities to become persons of worth. Neither to venture into the rain herself nor to speak to those there would itself be an act of domination.

Notes

Introduction. The promise of cultural alternatives

1 Anthropologists compare their responses to those of other anthropologists and to those of the people whose lives they are investigating for several related reasons. Through such comparisons, they can appraise, and perhaps compensate for, the extent of their own cultural, personal and theoretical biases. See, for example, Rabinow, 1977; Crapanzano, 1980; Dwyer, 1982; Errington 1984; and Strathern, 1984 for efforts to understand the effect on fieldwork of the ethnographer's expectations. Other recent studies such as Bovin, 1966; Wax, 1979; Gonzalez 1984; and Gregory, 1984 examine the effects on fieldwork of the ethnographer's sex.

As a result of such comparisons, anthropologists are better able to recognize not only their particular preconceptions but the more inclusive set of cultural and theoretical assumptions which inform their system of thought. With the latter recognition, a variety of specific errors in interpretation can, to some extent, be anticipated and avoided. Thus, as one anthropologist has recently suggested "[p]erhaps anthropology is ultimately saved from perpetual tautology by its dialectic with the social theories of those it studies" (Strathern, 1984: 14).

To the extent that such a process of anthropological reflexivity results in more accurate descriptions and interpretations of the sociocultural world of both self and other, we will be able to achieve a better understanding of those characteristics common to all humans and those which exist only within particular sociocultural systems. For discussions about what might be learned most generally about human life from comparisons of these systems see, among others, Etienne and Leacock, 1980; Rosaldo, 1980; Ortner and Whitehead, 1981; Strathern, 1981; Sacks, 1982; Bell, 1983 and Geertz, 1973 and 1983. Indeed, this topic is a major concern to us.

2 We employ the phonetic transcriptions of Chambri words provided by Mead and Fortune only when citing or discussing their writings.

3 That this hatchet had been given to his father in exchange for a decorated skull undoubtedly contributed to its meaning for Yorondu. Chambri, as we will discuss later in detail, regard all power as ancestral power. Through ritual activities, a man is able to embody power by *becoming* his ancestors – including his deceased father. Certain objects such as skulls also can contain this ancestral power. If this ancestral hatchet were regarded as comparable to such objects – and it had, after all, been received in exchange for a skull – then Yorondu may have been presenting us with more than a memento. Rather, in a fundamental way, he may have been giving us a portion of himself, a measure of his efficacy and his identity.

4 This discussion should not be construed as denying the importance of gender to a Western sense of identity. However, few of us wish to be regarded as primarily a male or primarily a female. A more complete discussion of the role played by gender, subjectivity, and individuality in the construction of American personal identity appears in the Conclusion. An additional difficulty in accepting the gender identity that the Chambri were applying to us stemmed from the fact that their views of gender, as will be seen, differ significantly from those prevalent in our own culture.

5 Both Deborah and her first husband acquired sexually ambiguous identities soon after they arrived among the Chambri. Deborah, in the course of successfully protesting the initial effort by Chambri men to exclude her from such male domains as the ceremonial house, demonstrated sufficient command of what Chambri regarded as male capacities for bluff and confrontation that she was regarded as, at least, partly male. She was, thus, able to escape many of the strictures of Chambri gender identity and was eventually given access to both male and female domains. In addition, her sexually ambiguous Chambri identity received confirmation from the fact that her husband was regarded as, at least, partly female: because he – a non-anthropologist – participated only sporadically in Chambri public life, he was seen as acting more like a woman than a man. Moreover, the Chambri view of each as sexually ambiguous received apparent confirmation from the fact that they had only one child, whereas sexually normal people of comparable ages would have had many more. (See Gewertz, 1984, for a more detailed discussion of these early negotiations with the Chambri about gender identity.) With Frederick's arrival and his display of what seemed to be more conventional male behavior, the Chambri attempted to make the sexual identities of those in the anthropological entourage less ambiguous. (See Douglas, 1966, for the classic anthropological statement on the cultural significance of sexual and other forms of ambiguity.)

6 A long tradition in Western thought holds that the form a society takes results from the nurture its children have received (see, for example,

Rousseau, 1974). The association made between fascist political systems and rigid child rearing practices (see Erikson, 1950; Benedict, 1946; Adorno, *et al.*, 1950) led many after the War to think that world peace would be fostered if children were allowed more freedom. Significantly, the first edition of Dr Spock's *Baby and Child Care* appeared in 1946.

7 The Women's Liberation Movement was, of course, the result of this perception. See such classics of the formative period as De Beauvoir, 1953; Friedan, 1964; Millett, 1978.

8 In Chapter 3, note 3, we discuss the production and sale of mosquito bags, and evaluate Mead's contention that Chambri women controlled the revenue from these sales. The shells acquired through the sale of these bags would have been of three kinds: *talimbun*, a green snail shell (*Turbo marmoratus*); *lin*, a bracelet or necklace that could consist of a string of different kinds of shells, including cowrie and conus; and *kina*, the goldlip pearl shell (*Pinctata margaritifera*). *Talimbun* was the most prized of the shell valuables.

9 Mead retained this perspective in her later works. For instance, in *New Lives for Old* she describes the ethos of Manus society as "an essentially masculine one, in which the protective capacities of the male, rather than the specifically maternal capacities of the female are the ones woven into the idea of parenthood. The ideal of personality is active, assertive, demanding, with great emphasis upon freedom of movement. There is likewise a very low interest in biological parenthood, in the breast-feeding tie between mother and child, or in any softness of feminine responsiveness which would yield too easily to evoke a measure of masculine anger" (1956:399). Thus, both Manus men and women are understood as having essentially the same personality configuration as Western men.

10 In the course of her career, Mead shifted her position slightly concerning the nature of the determinants of gender differences. In her earlier *Sex and Temperament* (1935) she argued that gender was entirely a cultural construction; later with the appearance of *Male and Female* (1949) she acknowledged that biological differences between males and females were likely to have some, although still very limited, effect on cultural definitions of gender.

11 One of the more important recent anthropological efforts to demonstrate the existence of such a universal human pattern appears in Spiro, 1979. Here he attempts to account for an ideological shift during several decades on an Israeli kibbutz in which the view that sex role assignments should be based on equality was replaced by the view that they should be based on equivalence. He suggests "that the kibbutz division of labor, in which men work in farming and women in nonfarming labor [such as childcare], is the result of innate sexual differences. Women ... are most fulfilled by working with and helping

other people, while men are most fulfilled when working with machinery and in tasks which give them a sense of power and domination" (1979: 19). His argument has been heavily criticized by reviewers such as Bowes, who writes: "Spiro simply fails to make his case. He isolates the kibbutz from its context, Israeli society; he ignores the historical specificity of the kibbutz...; he dismisses cultural factors far too easily, ignoring the wealth of cross-cultural literature on sex roles" (1981: 322). See also Cook, 1982 and Datan, 1981 for comparable views.

12 There is also an implication – one, admittedly, not central to the argument in this book – that a foreign policy which fosters economic intervention into the lives of non-Western peoples is justified since they are, after all, just like us in their aspirations (see Rostow, 1978, for example). Such a policy of modernization, however, in the view of many (see Stavenhagen, 1975; Frank, 1978; Taussig; 1980; and Meillassoux, 1981) leads to a condition of impoverished dependence upon Western nations.

13 It would, of course, be possible to argue that universal patterns of male and female behavior and dispositions exist which do *not* conform to Western cultural expectations about gender. However, as many authors such as Bleier, 1984, convincingly show, most attempts to demonstrate the existence of universal gender patterns do, in fact, take Western expectations as the model.

14 Important current research seeks to specify more accurately the various sociocultural mechanisms such as initiation (see, for example, Tuzin 1980; Herdt, 1981, 1982 and Poole, 1982), which bring an individual's sense of self further into line with the cultural definition of what persons are.

15 A more extensive discussion of culturally distinct concepts of person is presented in Chapter 2.

1. Entropy and the nature of indebtedness

1 Although the German Government established claim to what is now the East Sepik Province of Papua New Guinea in the late 19th century, the Chambri Lake region was not effectively controlled by Europeans until the Australian administration established regular patrols there in the mid 1920s.

2 Chambri frequently explain aspects of Chambri life by telling myths which justify contemporary action in terms of the past. Since, as we will make clear in Chapter 4 through our discussion of immanent totemism, living Chambri acquire power through becoming their ancestors, historical precedent is regarded as appropriately configuring the present. When myths are cited in debates, rarely will the accuracy with which events are depicted be contested; instead argu-

ment focuses on who has the right to become those ancestors described in the story.

3 Prior to the early 1960s, young men would leave Chambri for two-year periods, to work as plantation laborers, often in New Britain and New Ireland. At the end of their contracts, they would return home, marry and assume adult responsibilities. Now, when young men leave Chambri for work, no one is clear how long they will remain away. In some cases, it is likely that, aside from occasional visits home, they will stay away for the rest of their lives.

4 Chambri frequently use myths didactically, telling them as explanations of topics under discussion, often with the preamble: This is why we do such and such. The myths themselves are rarely explained. Indeed, a Chambri, if pressed by an ethnographer for explication of a myth, is likely to respond with confusion, perhaps simply saying, that's how things are or, sometimes, presenting yet another myth. Thus, myths, as explanations, do not seem to be regarded by the Chambri as themselves subject to explanation. Consequently, in order for us to explicate a Chambri myth – to elucidate the meaning of that which apparently strikes the Chambri as self-evident – we must proceed by interpreting it with reference to the particular context in which it was told as well as to the more general sociocultural context of Chambri concerns and expectations.

5 That the Chambri have a more unitary view of power – regarding it as more comprehensive in scope – than do we provides an illustration of Anderson's (1972) thesis (brilliantly argued with reference to sharply contrasting Western and Javanese examples) that concepts of power are subject to substantial cross-cultural variation.

6 An *uncheban* in unlike a totemic spirit. While the latter is an ancestor and is controlled by living humans, the former is not. Mandonk is thus, in contrast to the *uncheban*, fundamentally human.

7 This is not the only Chambri myth which illustrates the preoccupation with correct and incorrect marriage relationships. Deborah has analyzed another of these in Gewertz, 1983: 66–74.

8 The Chambri believe that conception occurs in the womb as menstrual blood and semen are shaped to form, respectively, the blood and the bones of the fetus by repeated acts of sexual intercourse. Men, at least, argue that the effective agent which does this shaping is the "wind" generated during intercourse. This "wind" produces an imprint of the father's patriclan on the fetus in a way analogous to the power of totemic names, when properly chanted, to shape the world.

9 An illegitimate Chambri child would not be in a situation comparable to this mythic child of the *uncheban*, for it would be readily incorporated into the patriclan of either of its biological parents.

10 That Yaproagwe can produce not only local kinds of fish from her body, but also those varieties of salt water clams and snails from which

kina and *talimbun* come, makes her fecundity all the more extraordinary.

11 As we will discuss in Chapter 3, the Chambri follow their preference for mother's brother's daughter's marriage some 30 per cent of the time. For this and any other form of marriage a bride-price and subsequent affinal payments are required. In addition, as we will later discuss, primarily in Chapter 6, the Chambri have patrimoieties that are supposed to be exogamous, although only about 60 per cent of marriages do, in fact, take place between clans of the opposite moiety.

12 In their view that human existence does not in itself confer personhood, the Chambri express a perspective which contrasts to the more universalistic ethic propounded within our own culture. Through reference to another New Guinea society with ethical views comparable to those of the Chambri, Read, 1955, explores this contrast in detail.

13 A discussion of the contrast between the pattern of perpetual indebtedness found among the Chambri and the oscillating indebtedness found in the New Guinea Highlands appears in Gewertz, 1977.

14 The predicament in which Wapiyeri found himself is analyzed in more detail in Gewertz, 1983: 185–189.

15 Chambri men, as will be amply documented, are exceedingly sensitive to any implication that their power is declining. Loss of power means not only an immediate loss of prestige but presages further loss of power, since men who have been weakened will be less able to defend themselves against their competitors. After a political reverse, men will do their utmost, with varying degrees of success, to maintain their reputations by denying that power has actually been lost.

16 Chapter 6 presents a detailed study of the process by which one clan is absorbed into – "goes inside" – another. Under these circumstances, the subject clan not only loses control over its estate, as mentioned, but eventually loses even a residual identity. This latter conclusion rests on the fact that in many cases the Chambri have only the most uncertain recollections of whether or not a clan has absorbed another: presumably, uncertain recollections become, with the further passage of time, no recollections at all.

17 Most Chambri political relationships, including those between father and son, are structured primarily according to relative power rather than relative authority. A father who has passed on his most powerful names to his son, for instance, would have lost the effective means to control him.

18 See Errington and Gewertz, 1987, for a further discussion of the competitive garbling of totemic names and the dilution and dissipation of totemic power.

19 Although we, of course, recognize entropy to be a term derived from the physical sciences, we could find no other which as accurately characterizes the Chambri belief that power is lost in the passage of

Certainly Chambri do experience inequality because they are indebted; and certainly Chambri are strongly motivated to shed their burden of indebtedness. It might be suggested, however, from these statements that although the Chambri are greatly concerned to achieve freedom from the kind of inequality that comes from debt, this does not itself mean that they are committed to achieve equality per se. In other words, there may be important sources of inequality which contrast in kind and in acceptability to the inequality which stems from indebtedness.

Some evidence does exist that argues against this latter possibility. In one important Chambri myth, for instance, a set of circumstances is depicted which precludes the generation of relationships of indebtedness. Significantly under these conditions, the men do form a society of equals. (See Chapter 4 for a more complete discussion of this myth.) In addition, as will be described later, the existence of a high degree of competition between fathers and sons and between brothers would seem to indicate that such differences as seniority and birth order do not themselves provide important or accepted sources of inequality.

2 Names and personal identity

1 In the decade before Papua New Guinea achieved its Independence in 1975, representatives of its various cultures were encouraged to perform traditional songs and dances at regional and national festivals in order to foster collective pride and unity.
2 The Chambri have adopted their totemic names from the neighboring Iatmul. These names translate for the Iatmul as, for instance, "Leg-fishhook-man" or "North-bank-earth-tree" (Bateson, 1933: 410). Among the Chambri, however, these same names are meaningless but are nonetheless still used to denote and invoke ancestors and their powers.
3 Thus, each year when the water from the Sepik River pours into Chambri Lake, everyone knows that this is because Yarapat, as the leader of his clan, has become his ancestor, Saun. Although some few others may know the names he employs to become Saun, as long as Yarapat's clan remains strong, no one would be likely to use them in an attempt to usurp his totemic role. An interloper would be unlikely to receive public recognition for his achievement and would, in addition, provoke private retribution through sorcery by Yarapat and his ancestors. However, if Yarapat and his clan were to decline in influence, they might also lose claims to totemic power since part of the process of becoming a client is the loss of totemic autonomy. If Yarapat's clan were to become absorbed, then the leader of the patron

clan would begin to act as Saun's descendant. Since, as we have said, Chambri do not keep extensive genealogies but base clan membership on the common ownership of totems, once a clan becomes a client, its totems as well as its ancestors are subsumed. In Chapter 6 we provide a case study of this process.

4 Few Chambri migrate as far as Port Moresby. In 1975, when Deborah encountered Kinsinkamboi, only six Chambri lived there.

5 Chambri believe that only those who are able clearly to envision and activate their totemic names and powers can sustain themselves as strong individuals away from home, especially when living among potentially hostile aliens. Travelers and migrants may, thus, through their survival abroad be able to prove themselves as men of power, men to be reckoned with, on their return home.

6 "Eagle Magic" is a particularly powerful form of sorcery, believed to have been learned by Chambri from the Tolai while working on plantations in New Britain.

7 Each of the three Chambri villages tends to be endogamous about 80 per cent of the time, according to census information Deborah collected in 1974. See Chapter 3, Table 1 for a more detailed tabulation.

8 Until Independence, the official currency of Papua New Guinea was the Australian dollar, denoted as "A$." Subsequently, the currency became the Papua New Guinea kina, denoted "K$."

9 See Errington, 1974b and 1984, and White and Kirkpatrick, 1985, for a further consideration of culturally contrasting modes of interpreting persons.

10 Kubusa beat a *garamut* or slit gong drum with totemically significant rhythms calling members of his patriclan to the men's house. The implication is that if he could summon the ancestors to speak through the drum, he could summon them for other purposes such as sorcery.

11 When Kubusa suggests that Yarapat had recently acquired his magic axe, he is implying that Yarapat has stolen it and is, thus, not entitled to this power.

12 Each of the three Chambri villages elects its own representative to the Gaui Local Government Council which allocates tax revenues for local projects. Although the Council has no power to enforce the peace, it does meet at Pagwi Patrol Post where a police detachment is stationed.

13 Again, all power, including that employed in sorcery, is acquired through use of names.

14 The Chambri are preoccupied with writing. As the debate excerpt indicates, David Massam, by transcribing a threat against Yaboli, was not just announcing his intention to attack. He was, indeed, attacking because the writing, as the embodiment of his thought, transformed his thought into a tangible and, hence, effective reality. When Edmund Maik said that "the words in the book did it all" he was not offering evidence of Massam's ill-will toward Yaboli, but rather introducing

proof that Massam had done the deed. The logic of this argument suggests what Levi-Strauss (1966) has described as the "science of the concrete," where the more embodied a phenomenon is, the more real it is – where the "really real" is no more than what it appears to be.

15 The government court adjudicates disagreements that involve accusations of sorcery, particularly when these result in physical attacks on people and property.

16 Timbunmeri is an island within Chambri Lake which has been inhabited since 1943 by Iatmul, originally from the village of Kandingai. Although Wapiyeri invited them to seek refuge there from Japanese attacks, they have, from the Chambri perspective, greatly outstayed their welcome.

17 Joseph Kambukwat's account of the wages he earned from the Public Works Department was an exaggeration. Indeed, he seemed to have inflated his own value throughout much of his account.

18 See note 6 above, about the formidability of the Tolai.

19 Ken Dowry has for many years owned a trade store and been engaged in a variety of enterprises at the Sepik River patrol post of Pagwi.

20 Michael Somare was the first Prime Minister of Papua New Guinea.

21 Largely inspired by Geertz's (1966) classic essay, *Person, Time and Conduct in Bali*, increasing numbers of anthropologists have come to argue that, in substantial measure and through a variety of processes, individuals come to understand and experience themselves in terms of the particular concepts provided by their specific cultures: thus, the experience of self becomes at least relatively commensurate with the cultural concept of person. In addition, such analyses demonstrate that for a variety of non-Western cultures, a person may be defined largely in terms of his or her social category and context (whatever the local definitions of these may be), rather than as, in our own culture, a unique subjectivity. See, for example, such recent works as Errington, 1974b and 1984; Rosaldo, 1980b; Geertz, 1983; Shweder and Levine 1984; White and Kirkpatrick, 1985; and Marsella, *et al.*, 1985.

22 It seems to us that an inquiry, such as Mead's, which seeks to understand Chambri experience must take into careful account the often implicit cultural assumptions which shape that experience – the assumptions through which Chambri experiencing takes place. (This is not to suggest that these assumptions are themselves not subject to change as a result of further experience.)

23 Mead's unpublished methodology and aspects of our discussion of it have appeared in Gewertz, 1984. We wish to thank the American Anthropological Association for permission to excerpt from this article.

3 *The enactment of power*

1 We have intentionally chosen a simple example to illustrate the difference between dominance and other forms of cultural constraint,

such as those applying to manners, clothing, and language. However, even these latter constraints which form, for most, the culture of everyday life can become the means of dominance. Thus, it is not an act of dominance for members of American society to be socialized to speak English; it is, however, at least arguable that immigrants to New York City from the American Commonwealth of Puerto Rico are being dominated over if their children are prevented from advancing academically because they are taught in English rather than in their native Spanish.

2 Marxists such as Braverman (1975), for instance, argue that under advanced capitalism workers are alienated from their humanity because they cannot adequately express themselves through work. Neither the conditions of their work nor the products of their work are sufficient to express their subjectivity. As regimented producers of partial products, they remain, themselves, incomplete. We return to this topic in our Conclusion.

3 Before the European introduction of cotton and nylon netting, cylindrical mosquito bags some 10 to 15 feet long were woven by Chambri women from sago shoots and bast. In Mead's view, these bags were the most important of Chambri trade items. However, it appears to us that the stone tools produced and widely traded by Chambri men were at least as important. We also must qualify her statement that women controlled the shell valuables received by their husbands from the sale of these bags. Based on Mead's observation that women did possess some valuables, Deborah suggested that these were the revenue from the sale of the mosquito bags (Gewertz, 1983: 91–92). We now think it likely that most of these valuables held by women were entrusted to them by their fathers at the time of marriage, to be given eventually to their sons. (Later in this chapter we present an excerpt from Mead's field notes in which she describes such a presentation of valuables as the "flash" given to a young bride, Mariabiendwon.) Since such valuables could only be used in the male realm of affinal exchange, we doubt that women would own many of them in their own right. Thus, as far as we can establish, Chambri men returned few, if any, of the shell valuables that they acquired in exchange for the mosquito bags woven by their wives or sisters. Yet, we think it inaccurate to assert that Chambri men alienated the products of female labour. No evidence exists suggesting that any Chambri man could do more than urge a woman to produce a bag for him. Whether a woman wove a bag to oblige a husband or brother or to please herself, she did not expect to earn shell valuables for her efforts.

4 The process of one clan absorbing another is described in detail in Chapter 6. Chapter 5 describes the process of acquiring control of the names of others through theft.

5 See Harrison, 1982, for an important discussion of the political use of totemic names in another Sepik society.

6 That Chambri women acquire worth through reproduction suggests a parallel with the circumstances described by Weiner, 1976, for the matrilineal Trobriand Islanders. In this influential analysis of Kiriwinan women and men she argues that women are of value as they reproduce the unchanging substance which gives matriclans their continuity, while men gain renown for themselves and their matriclans according to the degree of eminence they achieve through exchanges. The most theoretically significant of the many ethnographic differences between the matrilineal Kiriwinans and the patrilineal Chambri concerns the relationship between the objectives of men and of women. Among the Kiriwinans, both men and women share the same vision of the social whole but recognize that each has a distinctive role in the implementation of this shared society. Among the Chambri, both men and women pursue separate objectives and their society is a negotiated balance between the separate interests and strategies of each.

7 In Gewertz, 1984, Deborah argued that because Chambri women failed to participate in the politics of affinal exchange, they were acceding to a relationship in which they were subservient to Chambri men. After further research into, and analysis of, the respective strategies of Chambri men and women, this position no longer seems defensible.

8 This is not to say that men never do violence to women: Francis Yaboli, after all, did beat his wife. However, when men behave in this way, it is not as part of a strategy to establish power but, rather, indicates a loss of power. Nor is the occasional violence toward women part of a general male effort to control women.

9 Chambri men are much more frequently the targets of sorcery than are Chambri women. A woman is generally ensorcelled only in order to attack her male kinsmen. However, it is rarely clear whether the primary target is her affines or her agnates. Since the major purpose of sorcery is to demonstrate that power has shifted from the victim to the attacker, the ensorcellment of a woman is usually unsatisfactory because, in these cases, the identity of the true victim and, thus, the attacker is uncertain.

10 Even though there is general recognition that competition for power is inherent in the nature of Chambri political life, a man may, nonetheless, respond with (what seem to be) fear and anger to a loss of, or threat to, his power. It should be emphasized, however, that these emotions do not constitute evidence for the existence of a sense of subjectivity. Rather than, for instance, marking someone as distinct by virtue of a unique cluster of dispositions, capacities and perspectives, they are regarded as manifestations of human nature, as responses generally characteristic of persons.

11 A Chambri girl is most likely to be scarified if she has a wealthy mother's brother who wishes to display his resources by staging the ceremony.

12 A childless woman can achieve worth through adopting a child. However, for an adoption to be feasible, her husband must be sufficiently powerful to accept a relationship of debt, not only with the child's biological father but with the parents of the child's biological mother. The principal way that a man can dominate a woman is by preventing her from having descendants. As the enemy of her kinsmen, he can make her barren through sorcery (see note 9 above). As her husband, he can refuse to adopt a child for her.

13 As we stated in the Introduction, Chambri acquired shell valuables from the Iatmul who, in turn, traded for them from groups farther north. The range of influence of a Chambri big man was curtailed by the limited supply of shells available to his Iatmul trading partner. See Gewertz, 1983: 99–104, for a more detailed analysis.

14 The variation in degree of cooperation and solidarity among Chambri co-wives, which is described in Gewertz, 1983: 61–62, is in some measure a function of the clan membership of the women. The male propensity to marry around sometimes results in domestic arrangements where co-wives annoy and even dislike each other. This friction is far from inevitable and when it does occur is often resolved by building separate houses for the disputants. Moreover, none of these conflicts is so extreme that it results in one wife ensorcelling another, or otherwise diminishing the other's opportunity to redeem herself from ontological debts.

15 An old Chambri woman, if widowed, frequently lives with a son rather than returning to her own agnates.

16 Neither men nor women favor either the intergenerational exchange of sisters, as in father's sister's daughter's marriage, or the direct exchange of sisters. Indeed, only 2 per cent of the marriages Deborah recorded in 1974 were with members of father's sister's daughter's clans and no marriages involved the exchange of sisters. Such marriage systems are simply too balanced to appeal to Chambri men, who believe that neither arrangement would provide the opportunity for anyone to accumulate names and power. All men would be condemned equally to suffer the debilitating effects of entropy and could not strive to become the equal of their agnatic seniors. In addition, the presentation of a sister creates an obligation which, depending on demographic circumstances, a man may find difficult if not impossible to repay. Such a marriage pattern, therefore, would also make men dependent on the fertility of women rather than on their own political manipulations.

Although women are not caught up directly in the politics of affinal exchange, they also benefit from the present system in which men compete with each other. Male competition provides women with political autonomy: men fear women because of their capacity to steal male names. Moreover, as we shall demonstrate in later chapters, a woman's objectives that her children prosper are best served if her children have powerful agnates and matrilateral kin.

4 The construction of society

1 There is considerable variation, of course, in the degree to which societies make their indigenous political theory explicit. For two sharply contrasting non-Western cases see Errington, 1974b and 1984.

2 That myths convey new experiences in terms of pre-existing patterns of relationships is, of course, not unique to the Chambri. See Lawrence, 1964, and Errington, 1974a and b for documentation of this process.

3 A bailer shell necklace, called *kapompas* in Chambri, is frequently described as a string of shell breasts; a conus shell necklace, called *pinump*, is compared to a grass skirt; and a cowrie shell necklace, called *tugolurump*, denotes vaginas.

4 That Chambri men do not attempt to achieve equivalence through sister exchange (see Chapter 3, note 16) does not contradict the appeal of the Golden Girl whose significance comes from the fact that she *cannot* be exchanged.

5 Kevembuangga is, in these respects, comparable to the Chambri we have described, such as Francis Yaboli and Joseph Kambukwat. None derives identity through an inner subjectivity.

6 Members of each of the clans composing a particular moiety arrange themselves on the same end of the ceremonial house. Patrimoieties not only serve to unite clans socially and spatially, but, as we will see in Chapter 6, cosmologically.

7 Much of the discussion of the social relationships within the Wiarmanagwi men's house suggests Turner's 1969 treatment of the liminal period of ritual and the phase of human experience which he calls *communitas*. However, where Turner locates the appeal of *communitas* primarily in a universal need, we see the seclusion within the undifferentiated world of the men's house primarily as a retreat from the structural contradictions encountered by Chambri men as they attempt to acquire worth.

8 Soups are important in Chambri mythology and ritual for, among this people without a subjective definition of person, one is in a quite literal sense what one eats or does not eat. Women are transformed into birds and men into bats through consuming soup; however, Palimal and Malu, who avoided eating soup, remain as they were, free to use their magic shirts in their search for their wives. Although the ingredients of the two soups are not specified in the Golden Girl story, as is frequently the case in other myths, the transformative power probably comes from their totemic significance. Yepikanimbur, for instance, prepares her soup in a bowl called *Kamburulan*, which means "the *kambu* maker." Chambri would assume that she inherited this bowl as a member of her

patriclan, along with the ingredients of magical names she employs to metamorphize the women into *Kambu*. *Kambu* are significant to the Chambri since the calls of this species of bird are believed harbingers of death. In the case of this myth, it is the dissolution of Chambri society which these women effect in response to the male seclusion with the Golden Girl.

9 For analysis of the significance in terms of Chambri historical experience of the female flight to Kamchua as birds and the male flight to Suapmeri as bats, see Gewertz, 1985.

10 Because myths about alternative societies provide insight into indigenous ideas about social order and disorder, they can provide a productive focus for the comparison of cultures. See, for example, Errington and Gewertz, 1987c for a discussion of how the Chambri myth about the partial society of Tsimtsan differs in significance from the stories described by Bamberger, 1974. That these South American "myths of matriarchy" postulate alternative societies only to prove them unworkable, suggests a very different cultural view from the Chambri view regarding the relationship between male and female political strategies.

11 The implication of this statement is that, in the absence of a sexual division of labor, there is no division of labor at all at Tsimtsan. Such should, indeed, be the case, given the nature of the contrast between Chambri society – as it in fact exists – and Tsimtsan society. In the former instance, most of the non-sexual division of labor appears in the context of ritual and is the outcome of competition among men to acquire power and consequent eminence. This competition would presumably be absent in a society composed of women pursuing female strategies to achieve worth.

12 This male view that women can conceive through agency of the wind alone appears inconsistent with the aspect of Chambri conception theory that defines semen as necessary to the formation of fetal bones. Conception theories, however, are not always consistent. See, for example, Wagner, 1983.

13 The women living in Tsimtsan are still within a society. This is presumably the reason they are thought to produce normal children, while Mandonk's sister, Yaproagwe, living by herself, can produce only fish and the like.

14 The myth of *The Marriages of Mandonk's Sisters* contains somewhat comparable examples of behaviors that are, by virtue of their divergence from or reversal of normal patterns of conduct, clearly regarded as misguided.

15 A woman, for reasons to be discussed more fully in Chapter 5, is likely to overhear some of the secret names of her husband as he mutters in his sleep or performs rituals within the house.

16 That life in Tsimtsan is regarded as possible yet not very appealing to

women and that seclusion in the ceremonial house with such as the Golden Girl is not possible yet very appealing to men is more than an irony of Chambri life. It points to the fact that, as we have seen, the existence of society itself requires that men acquire wives but in so doing they encounter obligations which result in inequality. (*The Marriages of Mandonk's Sisters* presented in Chapter 1 is another mythic speculation on ways to escape the dilemma. See also Errington and Gewertz, 1985, for a presentation of a myth suggesting an incestuous sort of autonomy.) Women, in contrast, have little inherent difficulty in pursuing their interests. Consequently, the creation of a society which allows the unencumbered expression of their interests does not require the construction of a world sharply at variance to the quite satisfactory one in which they normally live.

5 *Politics and the relationship between husbands and wives*

1 Chambri characteristically provide explanations of topics under discussion through recourse to myths. Since, as mentioned previously, these myths are not themselves subject to further explication, the commentary that a myth makes about Chambri life remains embedded in the myth itself. Although the Chambri are reflexive about their culture, their understanding of themselves – including their understanding of the "logic" which comprises the internal connections of their culture – is conveyed primarily through illustration rather than through explicit analysis.

2 Kashibonga argues here that he and his family no longer have a relationship with Wenente, since they were never recompensed for the shell valuables they expended to acquire her for their *wau*, her first husband.

3 Because Kashibonga has become alienated from Wenente and her agnates, all Chambri would consider his interests in the investigation of her complaint about Ashkome's wife to be distinct from hers.

4 We do not imply that Chambri men never experience sexual jealousy. For us, and we suspect for them, a man's sense of sexual jealousy proceeds largely from a conviction that he has, in his identity, been diminished by a rival. However, the nature of the identity and therefore what is lost seem to differ in each case. For the Chambri, the adultery of a wife indicates that her husband has lost the power to hold her. If the husband is able under these circumstances to demand and receive compensation in the form of valuables from his wife's lover, he can reconstitute his identity by demonstrating that he has more power than his rival. For us, in contrast, adultery suggests that something has been found wanting in the subjective core of being, a suggestion that is not easily dismissed through success in political, economic or other forms of competition. A more complete discussion of the diffi-

culties in validating a subjectively defined self appears in the Conclusion.

5 A Chambri man will usually leave his patriclan for another, only if he believes his natal clan is at the point of losing its autonomy and if he can find a welcome in another clan.

6 We remind the reader that we retain Mead's spelling of Chambri names where referring directly to her data.

7 As a "runaway" adopted into Tanum's clan, Ashkome was initially in a weak position. As Ashkome's adopted brother, Taukumbank's position was doubly derivative and, thus, particularly weak. Both seem to have been especially alert for opportunities – indeed, opportunities at Tanum's expense – to establish themselves as men of power.

8 In addition, ritual objects have little intrinsic value which would make them subject to theft.

9 For comparable reasons, a Chambri woman will be attracted to a man even though he is completely enclosed by a *mwai* costume. These masked figures among the Iatmul and Chambri are described by Bateson as: "representations of totemic ancestors of the various clans. ... The boy or man inside the mask sings totemic name songs ... These dances have some courtship significance and the dancer inside the *mwai* sometimes suspends love charms on the mask" (1962: 7). See also Hauser-Schaublin, 1977, for a recent study of Iatmul *mwai* costumes.

10 At a 1986 Wenner-Gren Conference, "Sepik Culture History: Variation and Synthesis," Shirley Lindenbaum suggested that there appears to be a significant difference in the nature of political rhetoric between those Sepik societies where power is based on the control of secret knowledge and those New Guinea Highland societies where power is based on the control of tangible goods such as pigs and pearlshells. It seems to us that although bragging is characteristic in both areas, the importance of debating skills such as bluffing is more important in the Sepik. (See, Meggitt, 1974; Strathern, 1979; and Feil, 1984, for examples of rhetoric from the Highlands.)

11 Chambri state that a ritual object or, for that matter, a man may become feminized through contact with female fluids, even those fluids which are thought to exist within males prior to their initation. Thus, extreme care is taken to prevent the blood which flows from the many incisions administered to a young man during his scarification from falling upon any but his *tsambunwuro*. (See Gewertz, 1982.) It is at present, however, unclear to us why a flute feminized in this way – especially since this flute may already be regarded as female – could not provide an effective channel for a male ancestral manifestation.

12 Chambri women frequently invade a men's house during the initiation of young men and are at that time shown the secret flutes. This is perhaps a reenactment of the Golden Girl theme in which women

assert and men acknowledge that the interests of each cannot be met in isolation from the other.

13 Although a man appreciates receiving support from his wife, his main concern is that she not further the political efforts of his rivals.

14 For a comparative analysis of the kinds of strategies women may employ in order to influence men, see Lamphere, 1974. For a detailed case of such female strategies in another New Guinea society, see Strathern, 1972.

15 If her husband had been a more effectual male she probably would not have chosen to humiliate him in this way. For reasons that we shall see more clearly in Chapter 7, it is in the interests of a woman that her husband maintains those affinal relationships which will provide her children with well-disposed mother's brothers.

6 *The mutual dependence of brothers and sisters*

1 For recent studies of the circumstances in which the interests of brothers and sisters are seen as shared or as contrasting, see, for example, Strathern, 1972; Gailey, 1980; Shore, 1981; Sacks, 1982; and Feil, 1984.

2 Although a young man may have many who are the brothers of his mother, only one will act as his mother's brother – as his *wau*.

3 Even teenagers may remain with their remarried mothers, living on their stepfathers' clan lands. However, once a young man has been initiated he is likely to enter a household belonging to his own patriclan; in contrast, girls are likely to remain with their mothers until they marry.

4 Kinsinkamboi's father, Kabansebe, was Kambukwat's father's brother's son. When Kambukwat died and before their mothers remarried, Tadeos and Joseph were placed under Kabansebe's care until one night the adolescent Tadeos entered the mosquito net of Miamank, Kinsikamboi's wife. Kabansebe and Kinsinkamboi were both furious at what was assumed to be Tadeos' breach of clan etiquette, and many Chambri believe that Kabansebe's spirit retaliated by causing Tadeos' death.

5 The majority of Chambri are nominal Catholics.

6 This greeting by which older women pretend to be born of young women denotes unity through a collapse of generational difference. See Chapter 7 for a more complete discussion.

7 As we have stated, according to Chambri conception theory, the wind generated by men during sexual intercourse provides a fetus with patrilineal shape. When Tadeos' sister gathered what was left of his breath into herself she was, we suspect, expressing her identification with him as a member of his patrilineage – as a creation of the same wind.

8 Then Prime Minister Michael Somare is from the Murik Lakes of the East Sepik Province and was strongly supported by most Chambri as someone who understood their customs and who would look out for their interests. When Patrick Yarapat celebrated the completion of the large house in which Tadeos' funeral was later held, Mr Somare appeared as an honored guest.

9 Many ethnographers of the Sepik concur with Mead that people in this region are preoccupied with acquiring ritual complexes from their neighbors in order to augment their own power. (See for example, Schindlbeck, 1980, and Tuzin, 1980.) Although only Harrison, 1985, has thus far described another Sepik people as preoccupied with entropy, we surmise that, in as much as there is a regional concern for the acquisition of power, there may also be a regional recognition that power is diminishing over time. If this surmise is correct, it is necessary to consider how power can actually be imported. The Chambri, as we have mentioned, make a clear distinction between the power that may be invested in a ritual object and that object itself. Indeed, before they trade such an item to another group, they are careful to remove its power and, moreover, they will convey with it spells they claim are authentic but know are not authentic. Forge has described comparable practices among the Abelam (personal communication). How, then, can any of these people, aware of their own perfidious practices, not expect comparable treatment from their trading partners?

   A possible answer is that the intentions of those from whom an object was obtained are not relevant: If the object has the capacity to impress, then it is known to have power. The particular reason given to explain why the object manifests power may, however, vary among cultures. Tuzin, for instance, reports that the Ilahita Arapesh believe that any object which pleases them will also please their ancestral powers. Thus, these powers will choose to inhere in any "aesthetically" powerful object, regardless of its provenance or circumstances of acquisition (personal communication). For the Chambri, however, who believe that power is lost because the names which induce the ancestors to enter the realm of the living have been forgotten, the empowering of an imported object would proceed differently. While the Chambri might recognize that the names they acquired with an imported object were probably intended to be spurious, they, nonetheless, would be able to conclude that at least some of these names were effective in the Chambri context. It would, for instance, be entirely apparent to the totemic operator if these names were able to establish his identity with a Chambri ancestor. Others, as well, by examining the state of the natural and social world could appraise the relative power of these newly acquired names. (See Errington and Gewertz, 1987b, for a more complete discussion of this process of borrowing among the Chambri and their neighbors.)

10 Even though Yako would be a member of the opposite *nyeminimba* moiety, he has a *nyauinimba* name in this *nyauinimba* myth.

11 Yorondu was the only *nyeminimba* asked to perform. He had been invited to sing by Yarapat in recognition of the fact that he was Joseph's stepfather, and he especially enjoyed the chance to perform at a *nyaui-nimba* function because he could demonstrate that his ritual knowledge extended beyond the realm of direct concern to him.

12 Although male, these performers, particularly those playing the flutes, are speaking with the voices and concerns of women.

13 Yarapat did not revive the use of the Lokwi flutes themselves. However, by reuniting these flutes with the *sabulintoub*, he both demonstrated and augmented his power by recreating an impressive and effective vehicle for the transmission of ancestral power.

14 Gewertz, 1982, describes this phase of the initiation ceremony as involving sisters, mothers and wives. However, it is the sisters who are regarded as primarily responsible for the transformation of a novice, although they may be assisted by other women.

15 Chambri females have the same rites of passage for birth and death as do males, except in attenuated form. Furthermore, initiation for a girl takes place only if her mother's brother wishes to demonstrate his wealth by sponsoring the ceremony. Thus, as we argue later in this chapter, girls are established as members of a patriclan but are recognized as focusing their interests upon their relationships with other clans.

16 In these respects, Arione's sisters literally would make him into a man, and it is, therefore, important that their own incorporation occurs before that of his father and the father's wife. Without the initial assistance of his sisters – without, as the myth suggests, their becoming the parts of the ship's motor which provided Arione with the initial impetus he needed to defeat entropy – he would not have had sufficient power to incorporate his parents into his design. Arione's sisters, in other words, helped him gain the power necessary to supersede his parents.

17 As a meta-totem of the *nyeminimba* patrimoiety, the moon became opposed to the sun after European priests expressed their view that it was inappropriate for a social group to be organized under the emblem of a vulva. Today most Chambri refer to their moieties with the Neo-Melanesian terms, *mun* and *sun*.

18 The scarification of initiates is designed to remove sufficient mothers' blood from young men's bodies to ensure that they become strong members of their patriclans. If this view is consistent with the theory of conception (described in Chapter 1, note 8) that a child's bones are produced by its father's semen while its blood is produced by its mother's menstrual secretions, then scarification should increase the ratio of bone to blood. However, the Chambri know that even after scarification much of this maternal blood remains.

19 A Chambri shaman is possessed by a spirit of the opposite patrimoiety. S/he inherits this *wakan*, however, from an agnate, generally from his or her father, but occasionally from his or her paternal uncle. A shaman might, for example, be hired to determine through his or her *wakan* whether the disturbing dream his or her client had the night before actually portended the future, or whether it should simply be ignored. While in a trance induced by chewing many betel nuts, the shaman will speak directly with his or her spirit's voice, or will read messages sent through his or her blood by the spirit.

20 The Chambri prefer that the relative ages of the sons of a sister or sisters correspond to the relative ages of those who come to act as their mother's brothers. Thus, the first son born to a sister or sisters is allocated to the oldest brother, and so on. If possible, the Chambri also prefer that the man who acts as mother's brother be the full sibling of the child's mother. However, if a full brother is not available, then a half-brother or even an unrelated individual may act as *wau*.

21 Indeed, Tanum's power passed to his youngest son who was too young to have been a participant in these events.

22 The dilemma of retaining or handing on the prerogatives of political authority is a common feature of intergenerational transitions and has long been discussed in the anthropological literature. For classic considerations of this topic, see Fortes, 1953 and 1973; and Radcliffe-Brown, 1965a, b, and c.

23 A man will receive valuables from his sister's son at just the time he begins his major political push. As a member of the senior generation, he will then have just begun to inaugurate initiations and marriages.

24 Thus, for instance, as we shall see in detail in the next chapter, a brother will remind his sister's husband at the time of their marriage of the latter's obligations toward her. A brother may take insult if his sister is abused by her husband: he may decry him as a man of little worth and provide refuge for his sister.

25 A sister may, for instance, harangue her brother if he appears reluctant to sponsor the initiation of her son. A son is not an adult until initiated and therefore cannot marry nor effectively assist his mother.

26 Indeed, the eventual blindness of Kinsinkamboi's sister, Kubruk Alinsanagwi, was attributed by some to the revenge by Tadoes' spirit for his own death by Kabansebe.

7 *Marriage and the confluence of interests*

1 Since the advent of mission education Chambri have kept written records of those who have helped them in their affinal exchanges. They do this, they say, to ensure that those who contributed to the acquisition of a bride will receive an appropriate share of the bride-prices which the daughters she produces will eventually bring.

2 The money came from both men and women and from a variety of sources: from agnates, matrilateral kin and friends. Money donated from outside the clan would be repaid at comparable ceremonies when the donors were preparing to make payments to their own affines.

3 This individual is addressed as "father" but is not important enough to have the social position of "father" that a clan leader would have. See Chapter 6.

4 A "laplap" is a length of often brightly colored trade store material wrapped around the waist; a "meri blouse" is a voluminous garment made of similar material. Because both were introduced by early missionaries, their style is conservative by modern standards.

5 This use of fronds or leaves to enumerate and emphasize points is a standard feature of Chambri debating technique.

6 Despite this statement, no one considered Bibi's life to be in danger; nor would her agnates be likely to accept the bride-price they had received as compensation for any ill-treatment of her. However, that this statement could be made at all to wife-givers suggests that money has begun to change the nature of affinal transactions. We discuss these changes with respect to this and other situations in Chapter 8.

7 The *Luluai* in the early period of European contact was extremely powerful. Because his authorization was necessary before a man could work as a migrant laborer, he was able to extract payment from both Chambri wishing to work and European recruiters seeking labor. The *Luluai* was then, in this exceptional circumstance, able to translate his wealth into power through affinal presentations.

8 The bride-prices paid for Pekur's mother and grandmother could not have been in cash – certainly not in Kina. Pekur's conversion of valuables into Kina could only have been of the most approximate sort. However, some basis for comparing his achievement to that of his predecessors had to be established.

8 The monetization of social relationships

1 We in America, in contrast, who define ourselves as unique subjectivities and who believe in evolution as progressive development, attempt to acquire worth by successfully differentiating ourselves from those who have caused us. While the Chambri are preoccupied with paying their ontological debts and establishing social identity, we are preoccupied with self-expression and individuality. The Conclusion contains an elaboration of this contrast and a more complete discussion of the American perspective.

2 We have found the Marxist differentiation between a pre-capitalist and a capitalist economic system useful in characterizing this possible direction of change. In most pre-capitalist societies, producers establish relationships through the goods they exchange: because these

goods contain aspects of those who produced them, the goods are, therefore, valued as social persons, or at least as tokens of social persons. (See, for example, Munn 1977; Damon, 1980; and Battaglia, 1983.) In capitalist societies, by comparison, no social relationships result through the acquisition of objects for money, and the owner gains disposal rights over that which s/he has purchased, irrespective of how or by whom it was produced. Gregory, in his discussion of the mixed political economy now prevalent throughout Papua New Guinea, summarizes this contrast in the following way. "The distinction between gifts and commodities manifests itself as a difference between the exchange relation established: gift-exchange establishes a relation between the transactors, while commodity-exchange establishes a relation between the objects transacted" (1982: 42).

3 Parallels to the process of modernization as it has begun to be experienced by the Chambri have been documented all over the world. For some excellent recent studies see Etienne and Leacock, 1980; Taussig, 1980; Gregory, 1982; and Wolf, 1982.

4 Life in town is expensive. A Chambri family living at Kreer Camp in Wewak during 1983, for instance, was paying monthly rent of $K10.00 to those who owned the land on which the settlement had been built. In addition, we calculate on the basis of the consumer price index for the last quarter of 1983 that a family of four would spend a minumum of $K100.00 per month for a subsistence fare of tinned mackerel and rice, and most would spend considerably more than this to purchase such popular items as beer, biscuits, and betel nut (Shadlow, 1984). There was, as well, the cost of water, utensils, fuel, clothing and school fees. The minimum urban monthly wage of slightly less than $K140.00 – which few Chambri who attempted to support themselves through the sale of artifacts could earn – would be barely enough to meet these costs, and would certainly be insufficient to allow anyone to save much money.

5 Extrapolating from data presented by Jackson, 1981, we estimate that the joint income of Clemence Akaman and his wife was approximately $K110.00 per week.

6 It is through initiation that older men socially reproduce themselves. They transform young men – who have no access to the ceremonial houses nor knowledge of the names which enliven the sacred accoutrements sometimes stored there – into adult males. Once initiated, Chambri males are granted the privileges of adult status, while expected, in turn, to fulfill appropriate adult responsibilities, particularly those concerned with affinal exchanges. They can now marry, thus obligating themselves to their wife-givers, while at the same time they must also assist their clansmen in meeting the group's affinal debts. Initiation thus results in the reproduction of two interrelated relationships. As marriage partners, young men indebt themselves and

their clansmen to their affines; as productive clansmen, they help to pay the debts that they and their agnates incur through marriage.

7 The cost of travel and tourist accommodation in Papua New Guinea is high by international standards. As Wheeler suggests, you "can make two unfortunate generalizations about accommodation in PNG: there's not enough of it and what there is costs too much" (1981: 43). He also warns that "shoddy is the ideal word to apply to some places in PNG and even in those that are really quite OK, value-for-money is a tag you'll have little cause to use" (1981: 34).

8 In 1974, ten of the 39 dwellings in Indingai Village were large women's houses. These were still being built and provided the standard to which at least most aspired. Both in their size and in their significance, they dominated the landscape. In 1983, three large women's houses remained in Indingai Village out of a total of 46 houses. Everyone now recognizes that it would be an extraordinary event for a large house to be again constructed not only because of the expense involved but also because few would choose to live in such a building.

9 One of a husband's motives for so separating his wives is to make it more difficult for them to compare what he has given each.

10 Young men in each of the three Chambri villages have organized themselves into string bands which frequently compete with each other and also provide entertainment at all-night dances. Called "six to sixes," these dances are extremely annoying to those older Chambri who think them an inadequate substitute for all-night debates. At one Indingai Village meeting, several older men complained about the noise and one parodied the gyrations of a guitar player. Others suggested that a clubhouse be built – and at some distance from the village – to better seclude these parties. Other Sepik communities indeed, have constructed such clubhouses which often combine the features of traditional men's houses with those of hotel bars.

11 Yorondu counts as an important part of his totemic knowledge his spells for pulling money: his "dog power" fetches the money; his "chicken power" scatches up the money; his "coconut power" makes money fall from the sky; his "pig power" scares the money so that it will not hide. Yorondu was in fact disappointed that his magic was so evidently insufficient to provide him with money but comforted himself by saying that he had pulled us to Chambri and we had money.

12 Akapina's husband had been Wapiyeri's younger brother. At the time that she moved to Wewak, Wapiyeri's clan was still experiencing the difficulties which we described in Chapter 1.

13 Lucas was thus acknowledging a degree of debt to Akapina's agnates – because they were in some sense his affines – and to her husband's agnates – since they had paid bride-price for her.

14 It is, however, beyond our immediate concern here to discuss in detail the relationship between the introduction of a generalized medium of

exchange and the development of a concept of person which focuses on an individual subjectivity.

15 As of this writing, the *Salvinia molesta* which has made subsistence so difficult since 1977 appears to be nearly under control by an introduced weevil. Philip Thomas, the coordinator of the control project, wrote us in 1984 that the weevil, *Cyrtobagous singularis*, is "doing extremely well in the Sepik ... Insects are now well established in the lake and, given a year or so, most of the *Salvinia* should vanish." Thus, if migrant Chambri do return to their home villages they will not starve. However, they may still have difficulty earning money there. The elimination of the *Salvinia* from the waterways does not, for instance, guarantee that tourists will return in numbers comparable to those of the mid 1970s. (See note 7, above.)

16 In the West we resist the idea that all social relationships can be measured in money. There is, for instance, the effort to distinguish between the impersonal social relationships of commerce and those of family and friends. Money, thus we are told, cannot buy us love.

17 The following table describes the 24 marriages which were contracted by Indingai men and women between August, 1979 and December, 1983:

Table 2
Recent marriages contracted by Indingai

	Men	Women	Total
Indingai	3	3	6
Kilimbit	5	0	5
Wombun	1	1	2
Iatmul	1	2	3
Sepik Hills	1	0	1
Others from East Sepik Province	2	3	5
Others	1	1	2
Total	14	10	24

Thus, during this period, Indingai women married Indingai men 30 per cent of the time; they married Chambri men 40 per cent of the time; and they married non-Chambri 60 per cent of the time. Indingai men, on the other hand, married women of their village 22 per cent of the time; they married Chambri women 64 per cent of the time; and married non-Chambri 35 per cent of the time. In addition, three young women, including Lucy, bore illegitimate children to non-Chambri.

18 Since Vatican Two, many of the Catholic missionaries have adopted a liberalized policy which views socioeconomic development as a significant objective of church policy.

19 Novels, such as these, not only help individuals to understand their own special subjectivities – and those of others – but are among the many cultural mechanisms which lead individuals to regard themselves and others as having a subjective self. See Watt, 1959, for an excellent discussion of the sociohistorical process whereby persons became defined and experienced as having subjective selves and, concomitantly, the literary form of the novel was produced.

Conclusion   The significance of cultural alternatives

1 We wish to thank Marilyn Strathern for calling our attention to this cartoon during a symposium entitled *Gender Relations* at the 1984 meetings of the Australia and New Zealand Association for the Advancement of Science.

2 Thus anthropologists commonly discover that it is virtually impossible for them to explain to those among whom they are doing field work that they wish occasional privacy to reconstitute themselves. In cultures where the self is primarily public and social, a desire simply to be alone is likely to be regarded either as incomprehensible or as a form of antisocial behavior.

3 For a recent historical survey of the considerable literature examining the Western concept of self, see Johnson, 1985. We emphasize, however, that since we are undertaking to elucidate the cultural concepts which determine, or at least strongly affect, the experience of self and others we will remain as "experience-near" (see Geertz, 1983: 57) in our concepts as possible. In our efforts to understand the nature of this aspect of American experience we have been assisted by such relatively comprehensive sources as: Riesman, 1961; Henry, 1963; Slater, 1976; Varenne, 1977; Lasch, 1979, 1984 and Bellah, *et al.*, 1986.

4 We recognize of course that there are class differences in the form aspirations take but nonetheless contend that the desire to be distinctive is widespread. When Marlon Brando, for instance, in *On the Waterfront*, reproaches his brother for having made him throw a fight by saying "I could have been a contender," he is lamenting what seems to him a lost chance to be strikingly unique (Kazan, 1954). For a fascinating discussion of the effect of class in shaping efforts to achieve distinction, see Bourdieu, 1984.

5 Gilligan, 1982, for instance, has pointed out that the criteria of maturity that are applied to both men and women are generally based on the stages characteristic of the male life cycle. As a consequence women are frequently judged by standards that do not do justice to their own experiences, competencies and values. Without taking issue with this perspective, we wish to describe the broad sociocultural power that accrues to individuality as definitive of adult worth.

6 That an adult may be poorly regarded if s/he is considered childish does not, of course, mean that actual children are so appraised. Nor does this necessarily mean that poorly regarded adults are seen primarily as childish. However, without attempting to present a general theory of deviance here, it should be noted that such adults are likely to be thought of as imperfectly socialized – that is, as having failed to make the proper transition from childhood to adulthood.

7 We recognize that the actual process by which an individual interprets these appraisals by others of himself or herself is in fact, complex. See, for example, Cooley, 1902 and Mead, 1934.

8 Although a strike is a collective action, it is engaged in by individuals who regard themselves as having a set of worthwhile skills. Moreover, as strikers, they may in addition regard themselves as having valued personal strengths. In this latter regard, the choice that the labor song "Which Side Are You On?" presents in its lyric, "Will you be a lousy scab or will you be a man?," suggests that this form of collective action is also a measure of an individual's self-esteem. (See Almanac Singers, 1955.)

9 Sometimes, of course, people get jobs for which they are not well qualified. In this case merit is still conferred but may be regarded by some as misplaced.

10 Francine Blau, in a recent review of the condition of women in the labor force writes: "Primary determinants of a woman's decision to enter the labor force are the availability and level of alternative sources of income. It is primarily for this reason that women who are married, with husbands present, are less likely to work outside the home than single, separated or divorced women" (1984: 305). Blau also says that women are less likely to keep their jobs than men since women bear a "disproportionate share of unemployment ... [and that the] adverse effect of periods of high unemployment on women cannot be overemphasized" (1984: 312).

Summarizing statistics published by the U.S. Department of Labor in *Employment and Earnings* (Jan. 1983) concerning the distribution of female and male workers by major occupation, Blau finds: "In 1982, 71 per cent of male white-collar workers (31 per cent of all working men) were in either professional/technical or managerial jobs, whereas only 31 per cent of female white-collar workers (25 per cent of all working women) were in these categories. Furthermore, while a somewhat higher proportion of women than men were employed as professional or technical workers, over half of the women in this category were concentrated in the traditionally female fields of librarian; registered nurse; preschool, elementary, or secondary school teacher; and social worker. A substantial 52 per cent of female white-collar workers (34 per cent of all employed women) were working in clerical jobs" (1984: 306).

Summarizing statistics of the U.S. Department of Commerce in

Money Income and Poverty Status of Persons in the United States: 1981, Blau also characterizes the earnings of women by stating: "The median earnings of women who work year-round and full-time was 64 per cent of that of men in 1955 and fell to 59 per cent in 1981.... Sex differences in educational attainment do not explain this large pay gap. Even within educational categories women earn substantially less than men. For example, in 1981, among those with four years of high school, the median income of full-time, year-round women workers was 60 per cent that of men, while among those with four or more years of college it was 63 per cent. Nor are these earning differentials by sex primarily due to sex differences in major occupation groups. In 1981, the median income of full-time, year-round women workers was 64 per cent of that of men for professional and technical workers; 58 per cent for managers, officials, and proprietors; 62 per cent for clerical workers; 50 per cent for sales workers; 64 per cent for craft and kindred workers; 61 per cent for operatives; and 58 per cent for service workers ... [T]he sex differential in earnings exceeds what could be expected to result from sex differentials in experience and tenure. A growing body of research into the question of male–female pay differences supports the view that discrimination accounts for a significant share of the differential – probably over half. This is impressive, because newly available data sets have permitted researchers to control for a wide array of productivity-related factors in reaching this conclusion, including formal education, work history, and labor force attachment" (1984: 308–309).

11 We employ Bujra's terms of "non-work" in our subsequent discussion because it conveys the distinction of central importance to us between paid labor in the public realm and unpaid labor in the domestic realm. The particular contribution of domestic labor to capitalism is a matter of considerable debate which focuses upon whether the home produces commodities for exchange, labor power, or products for use by the family. However, even if it is the case, as some engaged in this debate contend, that women's domestic labor is work disguised as non-work by capitalist ideology, it is the sociocultural importance of the disguise which concerns us here. For the exposition of this range of views, see Gerstein, 1973; Seccombe, 1974 and 1975; Coulson, *et al.*, 1975; Gardiner, 1975; Himmelwait and Mohun, 1977; and Malos, 1980.

12 Summarizing data collected from 25 middle American families living in the Boston area, Lein states "[I]n the two-worker families ... women's paid work was seen as 'helping out' the wage-earner rather than as a change in the primary responsibilities of husband and wife" (1984: 247). Indeed, as Fox and Hesse-Biber, in their summary of the data collected by themselves and others since 1975, state: "Current research indicates that employed women continue to bear primary responsibility for home and family ... and that they experience anxiety about failure in these roles ... Men, on the other hand, spend relatively small

amounts of time in housework – whether their wives are employed or not ... Moreover, women's household labor represents a great demand not just in the time required, but also in the pacing of those demands ... Tasks such as food preparation that are performed by women represent constant and recurrent demands. In contrast, the chores likely to be handled by males, such as house painting and repairs, are not only less frequently performed, but are also more flexibly scheduled. In addition, as a group, men tend to approach children and family in a more detached and nonemotional manner ... Hence, while ... both men and women in dual-job families [are overburdened] ... for women these burdens and conflicts are much greater both at home and at work" (1984: 181).

Tavris and Wade summarize the nature of these conflicts as a "dilemma at the heart of [women's] lives: how to strike a balance between the 'selfless' pleasures of giving and loving and the 'selfish' pleasures of finding your own way in the working world" (1984: 283). They refer to a study of professional women made in 1981 in which the women "reported feelings of 'being drained,' 'emotionally leached,' 'overwhelmed,' 'guilty.' One woman physician said: 'I come home and I just don't have anything to give to Paul – that is a terrible feeling. I feel that it's not worth it – I resent my job. Then I resent myself for being so damned conscientious – to give so much at work and have to be reserved at home.' " (1984: 283–284). In fact, it seems that professional women control "the extent of their career commitment to fit the circumstances of their family lives – how the husband's work was going, his income, the ages and number of children, the husband's support (or lack of it), and so on" (Tavris and Wade, 1984: 283). See Gerson, 1985, for a further discussion of the way that women struggle with these "hard choices."

13 This is not to say that all work is regarded as gratifying, but rather that in general work is regarded as more important than non-work. Nor is this to ignore the fact that for some purposes, such as the settlement of a divorce, retroactive attempts may be made to place a cash value on this form of non-work. Such a compensation does not mean, however, that the non-worker was receiving pay during the time that the marriage was intact.

14 Much advertising is based on the assertion that purchase of a particular product will give an edge in the competition with other women.

15 Thus, after a picnic we attended, Deborah was told as an aside by another woman guest that their hostess had chosen a needlessly expensive brand of food wrap. In this case, the stereotype of women as neighborhood gossips appeared substantiated. As competitors who must remain vigilant, rather than as workers engaged in the same occupation, women are not likely to engage in collective action or to have much sense of solidarity.

16 Many women, of course, may find themselves more preoccupied with the problems of everyday survival than with establishing eminence in domestic competition.

17 Because of this cultural expectation, lack of success in the area of work can be demoralizing for men. Thus the unemployed men who hung around *Tally's Corner* (Liebow, 1967) had, as failed workers, much lower self-esteem than did the competent non-working women with whom they lived.

18 It is not uncommon to hear men complain that their wives do little during the day while they have been away at work. Nor is it unusual for men who have to mind the kids and the house for a day to remark with surprise how much effort it has taken.

19 However, in a national sample of American households, only 19 per cent of the women interviewed said they wanted more help with the housework from their husbands (Tavris and Wade, 1984: 286). This response, when taken with the statistic presented earlier that men spend an average of 36 minutes a week on housework in contrast to the 26 hours a week of their employed wives, provides additional evidence that women derive important aspects of their identity from their domestic responsibilities.

20 If money indicates that something has a value, it also indicates that it has a price. Virtually everything in the West is believed to have a price except those relationships based on a form of personal commitment such as love and friendship. Thus we disapprove of those who marry for money, of women we believe to be "gold-diggers" and of prostitutes because they transform what should be personal relationships into commercial ones, which are subject to termination once payment stops.

21 As one of the housewives Ann Oakley interviewed stated: "I think looking after a house and a baby is a job. This feeling of wanting to switch off at six o'clock is saying, 'That's it for the day.' But it's also more than a job: you're totally involved with it: it's your own home and your own flesh and blood" (1976: 126). Or, as one of the working-class housewives in Marjorie Rice's sample stated: "I believe myself that one of the biggest difficulties ... [we] have is our husbands do not realize that we ever need any leisure time" (1980: 88).

22 Art is valued as the purely non-essential, the completely non-utilitarian. Thus when people say that they cannot live without art, they are suggesting that their subjectivities have become so developed that art has become as necessary to them as bread is for others.

23 A variety of studies have demonstrated that advertising is indeed effective in establishing and supporting gender stereotypes. See, for example, Tuchman, *et al.*, 1978; Goffman, 1979; and the film by Kilbourne, *et al.*, 1979.

24 Many women justify their decision to seek employment, not as a source of identity, but as a way to supplement family income. As the housewife

in Ann Oakley's sample explained: "If I worked it wouldn't be for myself, it'd be for *all* of us" (1976: 110).

25 Examples of male autonomy resting on female contingency abound: The business executive who urged his university-educated wife to leave her job so that she could provide the kind of home to which he could bring his associates and superiors; the professor, married to his graduate student, who persuaded her to assist him in his work rather than finish her degree; the laid-off male factory worker who abused his wife out of the humiliation he felt because she was employed and he was not, are all familiar instances.

26 As Dworkin writes: "The separate-but-equal model itself originates in the conviction that men and women could not stand on common human ground. The model originates in the effort to justify the subordination of women to men (and in the justification to perpetuate that subordination) by positing male and female natures so biologically different as to require social separation, socially antithetical paths, social life bifurcated by sex so that there are two cultures, one male, one female, coexisting in the same society" (1983: 202). In our view, therefore, female anti-feminists who defend relationships of inherent contingency by arguing that the private female domain is equal to the public male domain are not simply adhering to an alternative set of American cultural values but are suffering from false consciousness. False consciousness can be regarded as a form of domination: more specifically, it is the incapacity to recognize the fact and the means of dominance.

27 Depersonalization is often part of the process of domination through practices of discrimination. Those excluded from access to significant resources are frequently described both categorically and negatively. Thus, all members of a particular racial, religious, cultural, occupational or gender group may be portrayed as animal, as excrement, as genital.

28 There may be more than one standard of worth within a culture, whereby members of a social category may meet the cultural definition of what their sort of person should be, but still define themselves and/or be defined by others as of much less value than the members of other categories within the society. That there is a more favorable definition of person to be found within a culture probably diminishes the amount of satisfaction possible to those bound by a less favorable definition of person: The satisfaction at being a latrine cleaner in Calcutta is likely to be curtailed by the realization of the way Sweepers are regarded by members of other castes. In such cases, domination is the restriction of favorable definitions of person to certain categories of individuals. See Errington and Gewertz, 1987, for a more complete discussion of cultural diversity in the bases, mechanisms, and forms of dominance, as well as in the ways dominance is experienced. (See also McDowell, 1984, and Strathern, 1984.)

29 Conversely, women who in fact are recognized as very good at demanding jobs are frequently regarded by both men and women as lacking femininity, as being inadequate as women. See Kanter, 1977.

30 Those in socially favored categories do not experience depersonalization because they do not regard themselves in categorical terms. Male executives, for example, do not regard each other as representative of males generally but do think of their female colleagues as representative of females. See Kanter, 1977, for illuminating discussion of stereotyping and "tokenism" in American corporations.

31 Domination may also characterize relationships of work, as we have suggested in Chapter 3. Nonetheless, work ordinarily does confer more value than non-work, and dominated male workers are likely to return home to dominate over their wives.

32 We repeat that in the American context separate cannot be equal.

33 Revolutionaries aspiring to create new kinds of persons may disagree with those feminist objectives which seek to enhance subjective worth. We, however, would question the morality and practicality of this objective of effecting changes in the fundamental nature of the experiencing entity: The people who would enact the revolution are unlikely either to frame or wish to respond to revolutionary aspirations unintelligible to them. Of course, if major changes do, in fact, take place in the criteria by which American men and women define personal worth then the nature of the contrast between the Chambri and ourselves would be very different.

34 The sense of responsibility to another simply because he or she is a human being is not likely to be characteristic of cultures with positional definitions of person. Thus, the Chambri could ceremonially slaughter infants acquired from the Sepik Hills without compunction because these infants had no significant social identity for them. See Read (1955) for an extended discussion of the relationship between ethics and concepts of person.

References

Adorno, Theodor, *et al.*, 1950 *The Authoritarian Personality* (New York, Harper and Row).

Almanac Singers, 1955 "Which side are you on?" In *The Original Talking Union and Other Union Songs* (New York, Folkways Records).

Anderson, Benedict, 1972 "The idea of power in Javanese culture," In *Culture and Politics in Indonesia*, ed. Claire Holt, *et al.* (Ithaca, Cornell University Press) pp. 1–69.

Bamberger, Joan, 1974 "The myth of matriarchy: why men rule in primitive society," In *Women, Culture and Society*, ed. Michelle Rosaldo and Louise Lamphere (Stanford, Stanford University Press) pp. 263–280.

Barth, Fredrik, 1975 *Ritual and Knowledge among the Baktaman of New Guinea* (New Haven, Yale University Press).

Bateson, Gregory, 1933 "Social structure of the Iatmul people," *Oceania* (1: 245–291, 401–53).
  1946 "Arts of the South Seas," *The Arts Bulletin* (2: 119–123).
  1958 *Naven* (Stanford, Stanford University Press).
  1962 "Notes on artifacts in the Museum of the Faculty of Archeology and Anthropology, University of Cambridge," unpublished manuscript.

Battaglia, Debbora, 1983 "Projecting personhood in Melanesia: the dialectics of artifact symbolism on Sabarl Island," *Man* (18: 289–304).

Beechey, W. 1977 "Some notes on female wage labour in capitalist production," *Capital and Class* (3:45–66).

Bell, Diane, 1983 *Daughters of the Dreaming* (Melbourne, McPhee Gribble).

Bellah, Robert, *et al.*, 1986 *Habits of the Heart* (New York, Harper and Row).

Benedict, Ruth, 1946 *The Chrysanthemum and the Sword* (Boston, Houghton Mifflin).

Blau, Francine D., 1984 "Women in the labor force: an overview," In

Women: A Feminist Perspective, ed. Jo Freeman (Palo Alto, California, Mayfield) pp. 297–315.

Bleier, Ruth, 1984   *Science and Gender* (New York, Pergamon Press).

Bourdieu, Pierre, 1984   *Distinction* (Cambridge, Harvard University Press).

Bovin, M., 1966   "The significance of the sex of the field worker for insights in the male and female worlds," *Ethnos* (31: 24–27).

Bowes, Alison, 1981   Review of *Gender and Culture* by Melford Spiro, *Man* (16:321–322).

Braverman, Harry, 1975   *Labor and Monopoly Capital: The Degradation of Work in the 20th Century* (New York, Monthly Review).

Bujra, Janet, 1978   "Introductory: female solidarity and the sexual division of labor," In *Women United, Women Divided*, ed. Patricia Caplan and Janet Bujra (London, Tavistock Publications) pp. 13–45.

Burridge, Kenelm, 1969   *New Heaven, New Earth* (New York, Schocken Books).

Chodorow, Nancy, 1971   "Being and doing: a cross-cultural examination of the socialization of males and females," In *Women in Sexist Society*, ed. Vivian Gornick and B. K. Moran (New York, Basic Books) pp. 173–197.

1974 "Family structure and feminine personality," In *Women, Culture and Society*, ed. Michelle Rosaldo and Louise Lamphere (Stanford, Stanford University Press) pp. 43–66.

1979   *The Reproduction of Mothering: Psychoanalysis and the Sociology of Gender* (Berkeley, University of California Press).

Cook, Edwin, 1982   Review of *Gender and Culture* by Melford Spiro, *American Anthropologist* (84: 422–424).

Cooley, C. H., 1902   *Human Nature and the Social Order* (New York, Scribners).

Coulson, Margaret, *et al.*, 1975   "The housewife and her labour under capitalism – a critique," *New Left Review* (89: 59–71).

Crapanzano, Vincent, 1980   *Tuhami* (Chicago, University of Chicago Press).

Daily Hampshire Gazette, 1985   Advertisement, Lands Design Corporation, Oct. 11, p. 28.

Damon, Fred H., 1980   "The kula and generalised exchange: considering some unconsidered aspects of the elementary structures of kinship," *Man* (15: 267–292).

Datan, Nancy, 1981   Review of *Gender and Culture* by Melford Spiro, *American Ethnologist* (8: 202–203).

De Beauvoir, Simone, 1953   *The Second Sex* (New York, Penguin Books).

Dinnerstein, Dorothy, 1976   *The Mermaid and the Minotaur* (New York, Harper and Row).

Douglas, Mary, 1966   *Purity and Danger* (London, Routledge and Kegan Paul).

Dumont, Louis, 1977 *From Mandeville to Marx* (Chicago, University of Chicago Press).

Dworkin, Andrea, 1983 *Right-Wing Women* (New York, G. P. Putnam's Sons).

Dwyer, Kevin, 1982 *Moroccan Dialogues* (Baltimore, Johns Hopkins University Press).

Erikson, Erik, 1950 *Childhood and Society* (New York, W. W. Norton).

Errington, Frederick, 1974a "Indigenous ideas of order, time and transition in a New Guinea cargo movement," *American Ethnologist* (1: 255–267).

1974b *Karavar: Masks and Power in a Melanesian Society* (Ithaca, Cornell University Press).

1984 *Manners and Meaning in West Sumatra: The Social Context of Consciousness* (New Haven, Yale University Press).

Errington, Frederick and Deborah Gewertz, 1985 "The chief of the Chambri: social change and cultural permeability among a New Guinea people," *American Ethnologist* (12: 422–454).

1987a "The remarriage of Yebiwali: a study of dominance and false consciousness in a non-western society," In *Dealing with Inequality*, ed. Marilyn Strathern (Cambridge, Cambridge University Press), in press.

1987b "The confluence of powers: entropy and importation among the Chambri," *Oceania*, in press.

1987c "Myths of matriarchy reexamined: The ideological components of social order," In *Myths of Matriarchy Reconsidered*, ed. Deborah Gewertz (Sydney, Oceania Monographs), in press.

Etienne, Mona, 1980 "Women and men, cloth and colonization: the transformation of production-distribution relations among the Baule," In *Women and Colonization*, eds. Mona Etienne and Eleanor Leacock (New York, Praeger) pp. 214–238.

Etienne, Mona and Eleanor Leacock, eds., 1980 *Women and Colonization* (New York, Praeger).

Feil, Daryl, 1984 *Ways of Exchange* (St Lucia, University of Queensland).

Forge, Anthony, 1972 "The golden fleece," *Man* (7: 527–540).

Fortes, Meyer, 1953 "The structure of unilineal descent groups," *American Anthropologist* (55: 17–41).

1973 "On the concept of the person among the Tallensi," In *La Notion de Personne en Afrique Noir*, ed. G. Dieterlen (Paris: Editions du CNRS).

Fortune, Reo, 1933a "Field notes," unpublished manuscript, University of Auckland.

1933b "A note on some forms of kinship structures," *Oceania* (2: 1–9).

Fox, Mary and Sharlene Hesse-Biber, 1984 *Women at Work* (Palo Alto, California, Mayfield).

Frank, Andre Gunder, 1978 *World Accumulation, 1492–1789* (London, Macmillan).

Freeman, Derek, 1983   *Margaret Mead and Samoa: The Making and Unmaking of an Anthropological Myth* (Cambridge, Harvard University Press).

Freud, Sigmund, 1925   "Some psychical consequences of the anatomical distinctions between the sexes," In *Standard Edition of the Complete Works*, Vol. 19, (London, Hogarth Press) pp. 241–260.

Friedan, Betty, 1964   *The Feminine Mystique* (New York, Dell).

Gailey, Christine, 1980   "Putting down sisters and wives: Tongan women and colonization," In *Women and Colonization*, eds. Mona Etienne and Eleanor Leacock (New York, Praeger) pp. 294–322.

Gardiner, Jean, 1975   "Women's domestic labor," *New Left Review* (89: 47–58).

Geertz, Clifford, 1966   *Person, Time and Conduct in Bali: An Essay in Cultural Analysis*, (New Haven, Yale Southeast Asia Program, Cultural Report Series, No. 14).

1973   *The Interpretation of Cultures* (New York, Basic Books).

1983   *Local Knowledge* (New York, Basic Books).

Gerson, Kathleen, 1985   *Hard Choices* (Berkeley, University of California Press).

Gerstein, Ira, 1973   "Domestic work and capitalism," *Radical America* (7: 101–128).

Gewertz, Deborah, 1977   "The politics of affinal exchange: Chambri as a client market," *Ethnology* (16: 285–298).

1982   "The father who bore me: the role of the Tsambunwuro during Chambri initiation ceremonies," In *Rituals of Manhood*, ed. Gilbert Herdt (Berkeley, University of California Press) pp. 286–320.

1983   *Sepik River Societies: A Historical Ethnography of the Chambri and their Neighbors* (New Haven, Yale University Press).

1984   "The Chambri view of persons: a critique of individualism in the works of Mead and Chodorow," *American Anthropologist* (86: 615–629).

1985   "The golden age revisited: a history of the Chambri between 1905 and 1927," In *History and Ethnohistory in Papua New Guinea*, ed. Edward Schieffelin and Deborah Gewertz (Sydney, Oceania Publications).

Gilligan, Carol, 1982   *In a Different Voice: Psychological Theory and Women's Development* (Cambridge, Harvard University Press).

Goffman, Erving, 1979   *Gender Advertisements* (Cambridge, Harvard University Press).

Gonzalez, Nancy L., 1984   "The anthropologist as female head of household," *Feminist Studies* (10: 97–114).

Gregory, Christopher, 1982   *Gifts and Commodities* (New York, Academic Press).

Gregory, James, 1984   "The myth of the male ethnographer and the woman's world," *American Anthropologist* (86: 316–327).

Harrison, Simon, 1982   *Stealing People's Names: Social Structure, Cosmology and Politics in a Sepik River Village*, Ph.D. Thesis, Australian National University.

1985 "Ritual hierarchy and secular equality in a Sepik river village," *American Ethnologist* (12: 413–426).

Hauser-Schaublin, Brigitta, 1977 *Mai-Maken der Iatmul, Papua New Guinea: Stil, Schnitzvorgang, Auftritt und Funktion* (Basel, Naturforschende Gesellschaft im Basel).

Henry, Jules, 1963 *Culture Against Man* (New York, Vintage).

Herdt, Gilbert, 1981 *Guardians of the Flutes* (New York, McGraw Hill).

1982 "Fetish and fantasy in Sambia initiation," In *Rituals of Manhood*, ed. Gilbert Herdt (Berkeley, University of California Press) pp. 44–98.

Himmelwait Susan and Simon Mohun, 1977 "Domestic labour and capital," *Cambridge Journal of Economics* (1: 15–31).

Jackson, Dudley, 1981 *The Distribution of Incomes in Papua New Guinea* (Port Moresby, National Planning Office).

Johnson, Frank, 1985 "The Western concept of self," In *Culture and Self*, ed. Anthony Marsella, *et al.* (New York, Tavistock) pp. 91–138.

Jorgensen, Dan, n.d. "The clear and the hidden: public and private aspects of self in Telefomin," unpublished manuscript.

Kanter, Rosabeth Moss, 1977 *Men and Women of the Corporation* (New York, Basic Books).

Kazan, Elia, 1954 *On the Waterfront* (Burbank, Columbia Pictures).

Kilbourne, Jean, *et al.*, 1979 *Killing Us Softly*, 16 mm film (Cambridge, Mass., Cambridge Documentary Films).

Lasch, Christopher, 1979 *The Culture of Narcissism* (New York, Warner). 1984 *The Minimal Self* (New York, Norton).

Lamphere, Louise, 1974 "Strategies, cooperation, and conflict among women in domestic groups," In *Women, Culture and Society*, ed. Michelle Rosaldo and Louis Lamphere (Stanford, Stanford University Press) pp. 97–112.

Lawrence, Peter, 1964 *Road Belong Cargo* (Manchester, Manchester University Press).

Lein, Laura, 1984 "Male participation in home life: impact of social supports and breadwinner responsibility on the allocation of tasks," In *Work and Family*, ed. Patricia Voydanoff (Palo Alto, California, Mayfield) pp. 242–250.

Leo, John, 1983 "Bursting the South Sea Bubble," *Time* (121: 50–52).

Levi-Strauss, Claude, 1966 *The Savage Mind* (Chicago, University of Chicago Press).

1969 *The Raw and the Cooked* (New York, Harper and Row).

Liebow, Elliot, 1967 *Tally's Corner* (Boston, Little Brown).

Lukes, Steven, 1973 *Individualism* (New York, Harper Torchbooks).

Macfarlane, Alan, 1978 *The Origins of English Individualism* (Cambridge, Cambridge University Press).

McDowell, Nancy, 1984 "Complementarity: the relationship between male and female in the East Sepik village of Bun, Papua New

Guinea," In *Rethinking Women's Roles: Perspectives from the Pacific*, eds. Denise O'Brien and Sharon Tiffany (Berkeley, University of California Press) pp. 32–52.

Malos, Ellen, 1980   *The Politics of Housework* (London, Allison and Busby).

Marcus, George and Michael Fischer, 1986   *Anthropology as Cultural Critique: An Experimental Moment in the Human Sciences* (Chicago, University of Chicago Press).

Marsella, Anthony, George DeVos and Francis Hsu, eds., 1985   *Culture and Self* (New York, Tavistock).

Mauss, Marcel, 1969   "L'âme, le nom at la personne," In *Oeuvres 2: Représentations Collectives et Diversité des Civilisations* (Paris, Les Editions de Minuit) pp. 131–135.

Mead, George Herbert, 1934   *Mind, Self, and Society* (Chicago, University of Chicago Press).

Mead, Margaret, 1933   "Field notes," unpublished manuscript, Library of Congress, Washington, D.C.

    1935   *Sex and Temperament in Three Primitive Societies* (New York, William Morrow and Company).

    1949   *Male and Female* (New York, William Morrow and Company).

    1956   *New Lives for Old* (New York, William Morrow and Company).

    1970   *The Mountain Arapesh: Arts and Supernaturalism* (Garden City, New York, Natural History Press).

    1972   *Blackberry Winter* (New York, William Morrow and Company).

Meggitt, Mervyn, 1974   "Pigs are our hearts," *Oceania* (44: 165–203).

Meillassoux, Claude, 1981   *Maidens, Meals and Money: Capitalism and the Domestic Economy* (Cambridge, Cambridge University Press).

Millett, Kate, 1978   *Sexual Politics* (New York, Ballantine).

Munn, Nancy, 1977   "The spatiotemporal transformations of Gawa canoes," *Journal de la Société des Oceanistes* (33: 39–54).

Oakley, Ann, 1976   *Women's Work* (New York, Vintage).

Ortner, Sherry and Harriet Whitehead, eds., 1981   *Sexual Meanings* (Cambridge, Cambridge University Press).

Philpott, Malcolm, 1972   *Economic Development in the Sepik River Basin* (Port Moresby, Department of Transport).

Poole, Fitz John Porter, 1982   "The ritual forging of identity: aspects of person and self in Bimin-Kuskusmin male initiation," In *Rituals of Manhood*, ed. Gilbert Herdt (Berkeley, University of California Press) pp. 99–154.

Rabinow, Paul, 1977   *Reflections on Fieldwork* (Berkeley, University of California Press).

Radcliffe-Brown, A. R., 1965a   "The mother's brother in South Africa," In *Structure and Function in Primitive Society* (New York, Free Press) pp. 15–31.

    1965b   "On joking relationships," In *Structure and Function in Primitive Society* (New York, Free Press) pp. 90–104.

1965c "A further note on joking relationships," In *Structure and Function in Primitive Society* (New York, Free Press) pp. 105–116.

Read, Kenneth, 1955 "Morality and the concept of person among the Gahuku-Gama," *Oceania* (25: 233–282).

Rice, Marjorie, 1980 "Working-class wives," In *The Politics of Housework*, ed. Ellen Malos (London, Allison and Busby) pp. 88–98.

Riesman, David, 1961 *The Lonely Crowd* (New Haven, Yale University Press).

Rosaldo, Michelle, 1980a "The use and abuse of anthropology: reflections on feminism and cross-cultural understanding," *Signs* (5: 389–417).

1980b *Knowledge and Passion: Ilongot Notions of Self and Society* (Cambridge, Cambridge University Press).

Rostow, Walt Whitman, 1978 *The World Economy: History and Prospect* (Austin, University of Texas Press).

Rousseau, Jean Jacques, 1974 *Emile* (New York, Dutton).

Sacks, Karen, 1982 *Sisters and Wives* (Urbana, University of Illinois Press).

Sahlins, Marshall, 19972 *Stone Age Economics* (Chicago, Aldine-Atherton).

Schindlbeck, Markus 1980 *Sago Bei Den Sawos* (Basel, Museum for Volkerkunde).

Seccombe, Wally, 1974 "The housewife and her labour under capitalism," *New Left Review* (83: 3–24).

1975 "Domestic labour – reply to critics," *New Left Review* (95: 85–96).

Shadlow, John, 1984 "Consumer price indexes, December quarter 1983" (Port Moresby, National Statistical Office).

Shore, Bradd, 1981 "Sexuality and gender in Samoa: conceptions and missed conceptions," In *Sexual Meanings*, eds. Sherry Ortner and Harriet Whitehead (Cambridge, Cambridge University Press), pp. 192–215.

Shweder, Richard and Robert Levine, eds., 1984 *Culture Theory* (Cambridge, Cambridge University Press).

Slater, Philip, 1968 *The Glory of Hera* (Boston, Beacon Press).

1976 *The Pursuit of Loneliness* (Boston, Beacon Press).

Spiro, Melford, 1979 *Gender and Culture: Kibbutz Women Revisited* (Durham, Duke University Press).

Spock, Benjamin, 1946 *The Common Sense Book of Baby and Child Care* (Toronto, Collins).

Stavenhagen, Rudolph, 1975 *Social Classes in Agrarian Societies* (Garden City, N.Y., Anchor Press).

Strathern, Andrew, 1979 *Ongka* (London, Duckworth).

Strathern, Marilyn, 1972 *Women In Between* (London, Seminar Press).

1981 "No nature, no culture: the Hagen case," In *Nature, Culture and*

Gender, ed. Marilyn Strathern, (Cambridge, Cambridge University Press) pp. 174–222.

1984   "Domesticity and the denigration of women," In *Rethinking Women's Roles: Perspectives from the Pacific*, eds. Denise O'Brien and Sharon Tiffany (Berkeley, University of California Press), pp. 13–31.

Taussig, Michael, 1980   *The Devil and Commodity Fetishism in South America* (Chapel Hill, University of North Carolina Press).

Tavris, Carol and Carol Wade, 1984   *The Longest War: Sex Differences in Perspective* (New York, Harcourt and Brace).

Tuchman, Gaye, *et al.*, eds., 1978   *Hearth and Home: Images of Women in the Mass Media* (Oxford, Oxford University Press).

Turner, Victor, 1969   *The Ritual Process* (Chicago, Aldine).

Tuzin, Donald, 1980   *The Voice of the Tambaran: Truth and Illusion in Ilahita Arapesh Religion* (Berkeley, University of California Press).

Varenne, Herve, 1977   *Americans Together* (New York, Teachers College Press).

Wagner, Roy, 1983   "The ends of innocence: conception and seduction among the Daribi of Karimui and the Barok of New Ireland," *Mankind* (14: 75–83).

Watt, Ian, 1959   *The Rise of the Novel* (Berkeley, University of California Press).

Wax, R. H., 1979   "Gender and age in fieldwork and fieldwork education: no good thing is done by any man alone," *Social Problems* (26: 509–522).

Weiner, Annette, 1976   *Women of Value, Men of Renown* (Austin, University of Texas Press).

1980   "Stability in banana leaves: colonization and women in Kiriwina, Trobriand Islands," In *Women and Colonization*, eds. Mona Etienne and Eleanor Leacock (New York, Praeger) pp. 270–293.

Wheeler, Tony, 1981   *Papua New Guinea, A Travel Survival Kit* (Victoria, Lonely Planet Publications).

White, Geoffrey and John Kirkpatrick, eds., 1985   *Person, Self and Experience* (Berkeley, University of California Press).

Wolf, Eric, 1982   *Europe and the People Without History* (Berkeley, University of California Press).

Index

club house, *vs.* men's house, 164n10
collective action, and individuals, 167n8
Coming of Age in Samoa (Mead), 9
conception, 146n8, 155n12, 158n7, 160n18
consumption, self-definition and, 132, 135–137
co-wives, 153n14, 164n9
cultural assumptions, and Chambri society, 12–13, 150n22, 155n10
cultural continuity, 131–132
cultural differences, 7–10, 131–132
Cyrtobagous singularis, 165n15

dead: ceremony for, 84, 86–89, 91; transformation of, 88
"Deja vue repeat quarrel", 71–3
depersonalization, 139, 171n27, 172n30
domestic labor: and capitalism, 168n11; compensation for, in marriage, 169n13; expression of rebellion and, 135; and leisure, 134; love and, 135; sex roles and, 168n12; as unpaid, 134; as validation of individuality, 134; and women, 133–134, 138; *see also* separate-but-equal model
domination: and American men and women, 139–140; Chambri male/female relationships and, 43, 48, 139–140; cultural perspectives on, 44–45; and definitions of persons, 171n28; false consciousness and, 171n26; by males, as non-inevitable, 140, 141; Mead's view on, 48, 52; other forms of cultural constraint and, 150n1; and well-formed lives, 138–141; work relationships and, 172n31
dual-job families, 169n12

Eagle Magic, 149n6
earnings, of men *vs.* women, 168n10
education: and pay scale, 168n10; *vs.* initiation, 113; and women, 126–127
ego differentiation, 42
elopement, 34
emotion, and identity, 152n10
employment reverse discrimination and, 140
endogamy, 55, 149n7
entropy, 28, 147n19, 159n9; *see also* power
equality: with agnatic seniors, 29; between American men and women, 140–41; Chambri and, 148n20; between Chambri men, 29; women's strategies for, 30
ethnocentrism, American, 9–10
European culture, and anthropologists, 1–2
European influence, on Chambri, 11–12
exchange: concept of person and, 165n14; and education, 113–115; gift *vs.*

commodity, 163n2; and initiation, 113; men's house and, 61; social relationships and, 163n2; *see also* affinal exchange; trade

female fluids, contact with, 157n11
feminism, Western, 10, 129–141
feminization, of objects, 157n11
fishing, *Salvinia molesta* and, 114
flash, 49, 96
flutes, secret: acquisition of, in myth, 89–91; brother–sister relation and, 89; Chambri women and, 157n12; female voice of, 160n12; in funeral ritual, 86–89, 91
formative experience, 35
Fortune, R., 1–2, 53, 94
Freeman, D., 9
Freud, S., 42
funeral bed, 87, 89
funeral customs, *see* dead, ceremony for; flutes, secret

Gaui Local Government Council, 149n12
gender patterns, as universal, 145n13
gender stereotype, advertising and, 170n23
generational difference, and women, 158n6
Golden-Girl myth, 57–62

health, 32–33
housework, *see* domestic labor
husbands, deprecation of wives by, 138

Iatmul people, 11, 148n2, 150n16, 153n13
identity: agnation and, 102; cultural context and, 150n21; and gender, 143n4; money and, 125–126; as positionally defined, 130–131, 172n34; and sexual ambiguity, 143n5; sexual jealousy and, 156n4; social definition of, 4; social transactions and, 39; as subjectively defined, 131–138; totemic names and, 31–43; *vs.* subjectivity, 35, 37–39
identity, Western, and class differences 166n4
immanent totemism, in art objects, 60–61, 79, 145n2
imported products, effect of, 11, 90
individuality: collective action and, 167n8; domination and, 138–141; and social contexts, 35, 37–38
individualizing influences, 119
inequality, Chambri society and, 148n20; *see also* affinal indebtedness
infanticide, 172n34
initiation, 113, 115; for girls, 160n15; social reproduction and, 163n6; women and, 160n14

intergenerational relations, 42, 52–53

jealousy, 156n4

kina, 24, 59, 144n8

labor: sexual division of, 64–67, 155n11; unpaid, 134, 168n11; *see also* domestic labor; non-work; work
leadership, 19, 29
leisure, and domestic work 134–135, 170n21
lin, 59, 144n8
Lokwi flutes, 91; *see also* flutes, secret
love, and domestic work, 135
Luluai, 162n7

Male and Female (Mead), 5–6, 14
male–female relationships: American, 130–141; Chambri, 7–9, 43, 48, 57–62, 139–140; *see also* domestic labor; domination; identity
male strategies, 57–67, 71, 94
Margaret Mead and Samoa: The Making and Unmaking of an Anthropological Myth (Freeman), 9
marking payment, 49
marriage: affinal obligations and, 105; arrangement of, 48–54; choice by women in, 55–56; as closed system, 52–53; and correct *vs.* incorrect relationships, 146n7; endogamous, 55, 149n7; father's sister's daughter's, 153n16; marital precedent and, 53–54; mother's brother's daughter's, 50, 51–53, 147n11; to non-Chambri, 124–125, 127, 165n17; opposition of women and, 99–106; outside home village, 54; ritual of, 99; sphere of clan influence and, 54; unity of men and, 99–106; in Wapiyeri's myth, 25; without bride-price, 34; *see also* affinal exchange; bride-price; remarriage
masked figures, *see mwai* costume
matrilineal society, 152n6
maturity, Western criteria for, 166n5
Mead, M.: on affinal preoccupation, 27; Chambri male/female relationships and, 7–9; on child marriage arrangements, 48–51; cultural assumptions and, 150n22; and cultural differences, 8–10, 129; and Freud, 42; gender identity and, 4, 144n10; influence on Americans, 5–7; interpretive error of, 7–9, 40–43; personality formation and, 40–41; research orientation of, 4–5, 8; and sexual fidelity, 73–74; and social responsibility, 8; view of dominance, 44, 45–46

men, American: and autonomy, 171n25; and beliefs about women, 137–138; domestic responsibility and, 168n12; and unemployment 170n17
men, Chambri: affinal preoccupation of, 27; and autonomy, 156n16; and Golden Girl myth, 59–60, 66; identity of, and ancestral power, 17; and objective validation, 137; partial society of, 57–62; psycho-sexual conflict in, 46; ritual secrets of, and women, 2–4
men's house: Chambri women and, 65, 157n12; and modern changes, 122; in myth, 64; social distinctions and, 60–61; totemic significance of, 60; *vs.* club house, 164n10
misfortune, 32
modernization, 145n12, 163n3; *see also* money
money: affinal relationships and, 111–128, 162n6; and personal identity, 125–126; totemic knowledge and, 164n11; *vs.* valuables, 111, 115, 125; Western relationships and, 165n16, 170n20
money tree, 58, 87
mosquito bags, control of revenue from, 144n8, 151n3
mother's brother, *see wau*
mother's brother's/sister's children link, 94
music, 87, 164n10; *see also* flutes, secret
mwai costume, and courtship, 157n9
myth: comparison of cultures and, 155n10; as explanation, 145n2; 146n4, 156n1

names, *see* totemic names
negotiation, of male/female interests, 71–82
non-work, as term, 168n11; *see also* domestic labor; work
novels, understanding of subjectivities and, 166n19

ontological debt, 111–128

patriclan, *see* clan
patrimony, 104
patrimoiety exogamy, 53
patronage, 26–27, 53; *see also* clans
person, nature of, 45, 47, 165n14, 172n34; *see also* identity; personal worth
personality: Chambri male–female relationships and, 43; as masculine *vs.* feminine, 144n9; non-reference to, 35
personal worth, 45; Chambri *vs.* American, 162n1; economic viability and, 45; "good job" criteria and, 133; objective validation of, 132; pay scale and, 133; Western criteria for, 172n33